Social Issues
in Literature

Race Relations
in Alan Paton's
Cry, the Beloved Country

Other Books in the Social Issues in Literature Series:

Social Issues
in Literature

Race Relations
in Alan Paton's
Cry, the Beloved Country

Dedria Bryfonski, Book Editor

GREENHAVEN PRESS
A part of Gale, Cengage Learning

GALE
CENGAGE Learning

Detroit • New York • San Francisco • New Haven, Conn • Waterville, Maine • London

Christine Nasso, *Publisher*
Elizabeth Des Chenes, *Managing Editor*

© 2009 Greenhaven Press, a part of Gale, Cengage Learning

Gale and Greenhaven Press are registered trademarks used herein under license.

For more information, contact:
Greenhaven Press
27500 Drake Rd.
Farmington Hills, MI 48331-3535
Or you can visit our Internet site at gale.cengage.com

For product information and technology assistance, contact us at

Gale Customer Support, 1-800-877-4253
For permission to use material from this text or product, submit all requests online at
www.cengage.com/permissions

Further permissions questions can be emailed to permissionrequest@cengage.com

Articles in Greenhaven Press anthologies are often edited for length to meet page requirements. In addition, original titles of these works are changed to clearly present the main thesis and to explicitly indicate the author's opinion. Every effort is made to ensure that Greenhaven Press accurately reflects the original intent of the authors. Every effort has been made to trace the owners of copyrighted material.

Cover image Terrence Spencer/Time Life Pictures/Getty Images.

LIBRARY OF CONGRESS CATALOGING-IN-PUBLICATION DATA

Race relations in Alan Paton's Cry, the beloved country / Dedria Bryfonski, book editor.
    p. cm. -- (Social issues in literature)
    Includes bibliographical references and index.
    ISBN 978-0-7377-4396-8
    ISBN 978-0-7377-4395-1 (pbk.)
    1. Paton, Alan. Cry, the beloved country. 2. Race relations in literature. 3. South Africa--In literature. I. Bryfonski, Dedria.
    PR9369.3.P37C7367 2009
    823'.914--dc22
                                                                    2009003282

Printed in the United States of America
1 2 3 4 5 6 7 13 12 11 10 09

Contents

Chapter 1: Background on Alan Paton

Peter F. Alexander

Paton was not only one of South Africa's most widely read novelists, but as a founder of the South African Liberal Party, he was also an important political figure. His early career as a warden in a prison school for black youths awakened him to the racial inequities present in South African society.

Contemporary Authors Online

Paton worked throughout his life for racial and social justice in South Africa. His first novel, *Cry, the Beloved Country*, is remarkable for its poetic use of language, sense of place, and call to social action.

Lewis Gannett

In his oft-cited introduction to *Cry, the Beloved Country*, Gannett relates how Paton's life experiences gave him the background and the spirit to write his extraordinary first novel.

Jonathan Paton

One of Paton's sons writes that although his father was opposed to didactic literature, his goal was to write books that would "stab South Africa in the conscience." Many of the views expressed by the character Arthur Jarvis in *Cry, the Beloved Country* are the views of Alan Paton himself.

Chapter 2: *Cry, the Beloved Country* and Race Relations

Chapter 3: Contemporary Perspectives on Race Relations in South Africa

Introduction

In the introduction to *Cry, the Beloved Country*, Alan Paton explains that "the story is not true, but considered as a social record it is the plain and simple truth." In lyric prose, Paton portrays conditions in South Africa in the early 1940s, when young men left tribal reserves to go to urban slums, where the lack of work and lack of traditional tribal structures led them to violence and crime. It was a landmark novel, selling around the world and bringing worldwide attention to the problems of racial segregation and white supremacy in South Africa. Paton has often been termed a didactic novelist, and he once said his motivation in writing was "to stab South Africa in the conscience."

While Paton was successful in attracting worldwide attention to the racial situation in South Africa, he was unsuccessful in changing conditions at home. Just three months after *Cry, the Beloved Country* was published, the Nationalist Party came into power and implemented a policy of apartheid, or legal separation of races. The racial inequality depicted in *Cry, the Beloved Country* was now officially sanctioned by the government, and a series of laws was put into place to separate the races and protect white supremacy. For the next forty-six years, the country that now calls itself the "Rainbow Nation" would be a pariah among nations for its racist policies. Many around the world wondered how this could happen and what would cause the development of such an inhumane system. To understand the world of South Africa depicted by Paton, it is necessary to understand South African history.

The concepts of white supremacy, slavery, and racial segregation came to the area now known as South Africa when the southern tip of it was settled in 1652 by the Dutch East India Company. Slaves were imported into the Cape Colony from East Africa and Malaysia. At first, the Dutch settlers lived without conflict with the Xhosa natives, who retreated farther into the interior of the land to avoid contact with the settlers. However, as the Dutch—who began calling themselves Afrikaners and began speaking Afrikaans, a colloquial language that evolved from Dutch—moved farther north, conflict among black natives and white Afrikaners broke out in the 1770s. The Xhosa lost these battles and became indentured servants to the Afrikaners. While land was set aside for the natives, it was inadequate for their needs.

During the Napoleonic Wars in the early nineteenth century, the British invaded the Cape Colonies and claimed them for the Crown, to keep them out of French hands. This created a new racial dynamic, as the British had a more pragmatic, less racially divisive, approach to the native tribes. In 1806, the British abolished slave trading and in 1833 abolished slavery in South Africa. Both actions created resentment among the Afrikaners and helped to promote the growth of Afrikaner nationalism. The abolition of slavery prompted ten thousand Afrikaners to vacate British territory in covered wagons in an exodus called the Great Trek of 1835. They settled in two new states that would be under their control and where they could continue the practice of slavery—the Transvaal and the Orange River Colony (later dubbed the Orange Free State). Along the way, they met resistance from native tribes such as the Ndebele and the Zulu, resulting in further black-white violence.

If there was ever any hope that the British and Afrikaners could divide up the South African territory, it was dashed by the discovery of diamonds and gold. These precious commodities were discovered in disputed territories and led to conflict. The result was the Anglo-Boer War, a war won eventually by the British in 1902. Britain was a magnanimous winner, quickly enfranchising the defeated Afrikaners. By 1910, the British decided to leave the Union of South Africa to self-rule.

Racial conflict and domination were an undeniable part of South Africa's history, but the British occupation had been relatively liberal. With the British out of the picture, the fiercely nationalistic Afrikaners, with their long history of white supremacy, began passing a series of laws to restrict rights for blacks and "coloureds," a term referring to those of mixed race. The Native Areas Acts of 1913 and 1936 relegated the African majority to native reserves, forcing roughly 85 to 90 percent of the population to live on less than 14 percent of the land. Voting rights were lost for black Africans in the 1930s, with coloureds losing their voting rights in the 1950s.

Behind these official policies of racial separation, there were some economic imperatives at work. The Anglo-Boer War and Great Trek had created conditions of economic hardship for many whites. Urban areas were crowded with thousands of poor whites, mostly Afrikaans-speaking, who were looking for employment. The government did studies of the "poor white" problem in 1906 and 1907. While differing conclusions were reached, most people were in agreement that the fundamental issue was economic competition between blacks and whites. According to George M. Frederickson in *White Supremacy: A Comparative Study in American and South African History*, the fundamental racial tension was "the crisis generated by the conflict between the demands of a newly augmented and insecure white working class and the established policy of capitalistic reliance on ultra-cheap African labor [which] led to a violent confrontation between capital and white labor."

Total separation of races wasn't possible due to the dependence of the economy on cheap labor from blacks, coloureds, and Indians. Apartheid focused on two specific areas—protecting racial inequality, especially in ways that would advantage the whites economically, and limiting the urbanization of Africans. When blacks lost their voting rights and were stripped of their citizenship, they became citizens of ten self-governed homelands in economically undesirable areas of South Africa.

At the time *Cry, the Beloved Country* was written, there were almost 12 million people in South Africa. Eight million were black, 2.5 million white, 1 million coloured, and a quarter million Indian. Three-fifths of the whites were Afrikaners. With a history of black-white conflict and minority status, Afrikaners sought protection in a system that legislated severe separation of races. As Mancur Olsen explains in *The Rise and Decline of Nations*:

> The system could not possibly survive for many generations unless the demarcation between the races was preserved. If less-favored groups could enter the more-favored groups, as they would have massive incentives to do, wage differentials could not be maintained. A continuation of the process that generated the coloured population would make the system untenable in the long run. . . . This is not only an implication of the [interest group] theory but evidently the conclusion of the South African government as well. Just as the restrictions on the use of South African labor in skilled and semi-skilled jobs increased over times, so did the rules separating the population into rigid racial categories and forbidding sexual relations, in marriage or otherwise, between them.

The conditions that led to separation of races and oppression of the black majority had its roots in fear—the fear that the Afrikaners minority had of the sheer numbers of blacks. If the playing field were leveled, the economic advantage they had could easily disappear. There was also fear of violence, for their history was one of interracial conflict. This fear is a major theme of *Cry, the Beloved Country*.

In the introduction to the novel, Paton writes, "It is my own belief that the only power which can resist the power of fear is the power of love. It's a weak thing and a tender thing;

men despise and deride it. But I look for the day when in South Africa we shall realize that the only lasting and worthwhile solution of our grave and profound problems lies not in the use of power, but in that understanding and compassion without which human life is an intolerable bondage, condemning us all to an existence of violence, misery and fear."

Paton died in 1988, six years too soon to see his dreams fulfilled with the dismantling of apartheid. However, the words of Nelson Mandela, as he spoke to the South African parliament in February 1999 about the healing process that must take place in South Africa under the framework of the Truth and Reconciliation Commission, are imbued with the same spirit of generosity as *Cry, the Beloved Country*:

> We think of those apartheid sought to imprison in the jails of hate and fear; those it infused with a false doctrine of superiority to justify their inhumanity to others. But we think too of those it conscripted or encouraged into machines of destruction, exacting a heavy toll among them in life and limb, and in a warped disregard for life and the trauma that goes with it.
>
> We think of the millions of South Africans who live in poverty, because of apartheid, disadvantaged and excluded from opportunity by the destruction of the past.
>
> We recall our terrible past so that we can deal with it, to forgive where forgiveness is necessary, without forgetting; to ensure that never again will such inhumanity tear us apart; and to move ourselves to eradicate a legacy that lurks dangerously as a threat to our democracy.

The articles that follow explore race relations and other themes as portrayed by Paton in *Cry, the Beloved Country* as well as examine aspects of race relations in postapartheid South Africa today.

Chronology

1903

Alan Stewart Paton is born on January 11 to Eunice and James Paton in Pietermaritzburg, South Africa.

1915

Paton enters high school at Maritzburg College.

1918

Paton graduates from high school.

1919

Paton becomes a science major at Natal University College (which later became the University of Natal).

1920

Paton's poem "To a Picture" is published in the college student magazine, *NUC*.

1923

Paton graduates from Natal University College with a bachelor of science degree with distinction in physics.

1924

As the president of the Students' Representative Council, Paton travels to the Imperial Conference of Students at London and Cambridge, his first trip out of South Africa.

1925

Paton becomes a teacher of mathematics and chemistry at Ixopo High School.

1927

Paton's friendship with Jan Hofmeyr, minister of education of South Africa, begins.

1928

Paton weds Doris Olive Francis on July 2. Shortly after the wedding, he takes a teaching post at his old high school, Maritzburg College.

1930

A son, David, is born to the Patons.

1931

Paton begins work on a novel he called *Brother Death*, which includes characters that would later reappear in *Cry, the Beloved Country*.

1934

Paton becomes seriously ill with enteric fever.

1935

Paton is appointed warden of Diepkloof Reformatory for African boys.

1936

A son, Jonathan, is born to the Patons. Paton joins the South African Institute of Race Relations.

1942

Paton is appointed to the Anglican Diocesan Commission to report on the church and race in South Africa.

1946

Taking a leave of absence to study penal institutions in Europe, the United States, and Canada, Paton conceives and begins writing *Cry, the Beloved Country* in a Trondheim, Norway, hotel.

1948

Cry, the Beloved Country is published by Charles Scribner's Sons. The National Party comes to power and introduces apartheid in South Africa. Paton resigns his position at Diepkloof Reformatory. Jan Hofmeyr dies.

1949

Lost in the Stars, a dramatization of *Cry, the Beloved Country*, opens on Broadway.

1953

Too Late the Phalarope is published by Charles Scribner's Sons. Paton helps to found the South African Liberal Party and serves as a vice president.

1955

The Land and People of South Africa, nonfiction for young adults, is published by Lippincott.

1956

South Africa in Transition is published by Charles Scribner's Sons.

1958

Paton becomes national president of the South African Liberal Party.

1960

A state of emergency is declared in South Africa on March 30. Paton travels to New York to receive the Freedom Award for 1960 from Freedom House. On his return, his passport is revoked.

1961

Tales from a Troubled Land, a collection of short stories, is published by Charles Scribner's Sons.

1964

Hofmeyr, a biography of his good friend, is published by Oxford University Press. *Sponono*, a play based on stories from *Tales from a Troubled Land*, is produced on Broadway and published by Charles Scribner's Sons.

1967

Paton's wife, Dorrie, dies in October. Paton enters a period of depression.

1968

The South African Liberal Party disbands due to the passing of a law that makes multiracial groups illegal.

1969

Paton marries his secretary, Anne Hopkins, in January. *For You Departed*, an autobiography, is published by Charles Scribner's Sons.

1970

Paton's passport is restored, allowing him to accept an honorary doctorate from Harvard University and to do research in England.

1973

Paton's *Apartheid and the Archbishop: The Life and Times of Geoffrey Clayton, Archbishop of Cape Town* is published by David Philip.

1975

Knocking on the Door: Shorter Writings is published by Charles Scribner's Sons.

1980

Towards the Mountain: An Autobiography is published by Charles Scribner's Sons.

1982

Ah, but Your Land Is Beautiful is published by Charles Scribner's Sons.

1988

Paton dies in April. *Journey Continued: An Autobiography,* is published by Charles Scribner's Sons.

1995

Songs of Africa: Collected Poems is published by Gecko Books.

Social Issues
in Literature

Background on
Alan Paton

The Life of Alan Paton

Peter F. Alexander

Peter F. Alexander is an associate professor of English at the University of New South Wales who is known for his biographies of British and South African authors. He is the author of Alan Paton: A Biography, Roy Campbell: A Critical Biography, *and* William Plomer: A Biography.

Alan Paton had an astonishing evolution from a housemaster who beat his students to a man who became a champion of prison reform, the founder of South Africa's Liberal Party, and the author of Cry, the Beloved Country, *according to Peter F. Alexander. In the following selection, Alexander credits Paton's father with having both negative and positive influences on his son's life. As a young man, Paton imitated the use of physical force his father employed in their household but eventually put this violence aside and embraced the deeply held religious beliefs he had learned from his father throughout his life. Alexander maintains Paton had a multifaceted talent, with the fame of* Cry, the Beloved Country *overshadowing the success of his other accomplishments.*

Alan Stewart Paton was born in Pietermaritzburg, the capital of Natal Province (now KwaZulu-Natal), on 11 January 1903. He was the eldest of four children, two boys and two girls. His mother, Eunice James Paton, was South African born of British stock; his father, James Paton, was a Scot who had immigrated to South Africa in 1895 and worked for the Supreme Court in Pietermaritzburg as a shorthand writer, a lowly post he kept all his working life. He was a tormented personality who influenced all his children, for good and ill, far more than their gentle, passive mother did.

Peter F. Alexander, "Alan Paton," in *Dictionary of Literary Biography, vol. 225, South African Writers*, edited by Paul A. Scanlon, Farmington Hills, MI: The Gale Group, 2000, pp. 328–45. Reproduced by permission of Gale, a part of Cengage Learning.

Paton's Father's Influence

Much of his influence was malign, for James Paton was a domineering and violent man who beat his children frequently and his wife occasionally. In the streets or in court he was a humble figure, noticeably short and habitually quiet; to the Zulus he met on his long walks in the countryside he was a figure of fun, a gnome of a man with a huge walrus moustache spreading below the flat cloth cap he usually wore. But in the small house in Pine Street he was a tyrant who, as Alan Paton recorded years later in his autobiography *Towards the Mountain*, "could make the whole household tremble." ... Paton described [his father's household regime] as "authoritarianism maintained by the use of physical force." Looking back from the vantage point of old age, he remarked of his father,

> His use of physical force never achieved anything but a useless obedience. But it had two important consequences. One was that my feelings towards him were almost those of hate. The other was that I grew up with an abhorrence of authoritarianism. ...

This abhorrence of authoritarianism, and the determination to resist it, he maintained all his life, and it is not too much to say that his life was largely shaped by it.

Yet, James Paton's influence was not all negative. Although his formal education had been cut short, he had a great love of literature, particularly the literature of Scotland; his children remembered his stories of Bonnie Prince Charlie [A claimant to the throne of England, Scotland, and Ireland, Charles Edward Stuart led an unsuccessful insurrection in Scotland, escaping into exile after it failed.] and Rob Roy [Robert Roy MacGregor, Scottish folk hero and outlaw] all their lives, and his vibrant readings from the writings of Sir Walter Scott and Robert Burns, delivered in the broad Glaswegian accent that he never lost, gave them a wide knowledge of these two writers even before they could read. James Paton also had a love of music, and he organized regular musical evenings to which he invited students from the local University College. . . .

Two further passions he passed on to his children. The first was a love of the countryside of Natal, to which he introduced them in long walks taken over the lovely hills that surround Pietermaritzburg. The second was a fervent religious belief. He had been brought up a Christadelphian but had parted company with the community in Pietermaritzburg when he married what they considered "a non-believer," for Eunice Paton had been brought up a Methodist. When his wife, and later all his children, became faithful Christadelphians, the community was willing to take James Paton back, but he spurned them.

The Influence of Religion

By way of compensation, he constructed a form of religion of his own in which he was the high priest, and his family the congregation. He decreed that Saturday was a holy day on which no profane activity was allowed. Even walking in the hills was forbidden. Yet, religious activity took up most of Sunday as well. In the morning the family would walk to the Christadelphian service, leaving behind James Paton and one child whose task it was to keep him company. When they returned from the long ceremony, there would be a family meal, the best of the week, and then James Paton would gather the children together in his bedroom for the service over which he presided.

Each of the children in turn, starting with Alan, would preach to him a sermon on a text assigned the previous week. The younger children gave only short commentaries. Alan's talks, however, were thoroughly prepared and carefully researched with the aid of concordances and commentaries. In later life he wrote a biography of the politician J.H. Hofmeyr [leader of Afrikaner Bond, a South African political party]

Alan Paton. The Library of Congress.

and remarked on Hofmeyr's having preached a sermon to his mother at the age of six; Paton did not mention that he himself had preached before his father at an even earlier age, and not once but many times.

As a result his own use of English, almost from the time he could read, was deeply imbued with the superb rhythms and cadences of the Authorized Version of the Bible, and his view of life was based on biblical morality. His father's trivial and humiliating rules he gradually shrugged off as the lesser moralities, but to the greater moralities, which he learned not from his father but from the Bible, he held to the end of his life. As he put it in *Towards the Mountain,*

> One did not lie or cheat. If the tram conductor did not come for the fare, you took it to him. One was not contemptuous of people because they were black or poor or illiterate. Justice was something that had to be done, no matter what the consequences. . . . Murder, theft, adultery, were terrible offences, but to be cold and indifferent to the needs of others was the greatest offence of all.

All these paternal influences played a part in Paton's life, and in particular his deeply held morality, together with the love of nature, comes out strongly in all his writing. . . .

Paton Becomes a Schoolteacher

He longed to become a doctor, but when he finished school with excellent results at the end of 1918 his father declined to pay the required fees for medical school, and he was obliged to seek a scholarship from the Provincial Department of Education, which meant that he had to become a schoolteacher. He decided to read for a science degree at University College, Pietermaritzburg, which later became Natal University, and though he went on living at home during his four years there, his father was obliged to allow him much more freedom. This he enjoyed to the full, joining in many of the activities of his university, and shining at acting, debating, the activities of the Students' Representative Council (a students' union), and those of the Student Christian Association (SCA). . . .

In 1925, having earned a bachelor of science degree and a teaching diploma, he was sent to the small farming town of Ixopo, as a housemaster in the high school there. At first he found the work daunting, and he was not a success with his pupils. Although the school was small and pupil numbers low, several of the older boys were only a few years younger than

Paton, and they were physically larger than him. As their housemaster he had to live with them, which meant that he was on the job twenty-four hours a day, and the strain gradually told. He considered his pupils undisciplined, and he was particularly shocked to find that the older boys and girls were allowed to be friendly with one another, touching and even kissing. His father's teaching had shown him only one way of dealing with this State of potential immorality: he began using the cane with energy, and he was soon feared and hated by the boys. The girls disliked him almost as much, for he turned on them his father's weapons of ridicule and humiliation. As a result, when he tried to persuade them to come with him to the annual SCA camp that year, none accepted. He would remain a master more respected than liked throughout his teaching career.

In Ixopo, which lies in beautiful rolling countryside, he continued the practice he had begun under his father's influence, of taking long walks over the hills, in part as a means of getting away from his pupils for a needed break. On the weekends he commonly walked twenty miles a day, and on many occasions accomplished thirty or even forty. These walks gave him the intimate knowledge of Ixopo's surroundings that he used to such effect in writing *Cry, the Beloved Country....*

Marriage and Literary Experiments

While in Ixopo, Paton met and fell in love with Doris Lusted. She was five years his senior, and she was married to a man who was dying of tuberculosis. Paton wooed her assiduously, and after her first husband died, he married her on 2 July 1928. The couple had two sons, David Francis and Jonathan Stewart. The marriage was not always easy, for Doris remained deeply attached to the memory of her first husband for several years, an attachment of which Paton was intensely jealous. Soon after the wedding he took a teaching post at his old high school, Maritzburg College.

His strong sense of the need to do something practical about the sufferings of the poor in South Africa showed itself in his active social work in Pietermaritzburg and in such poems as "The Hermit," which was first published in May 1931 in NUC [Natal University College] and later collected in *Knocking on the Door*. . . .

While teaching in Pietermaritzburg, Paton first experimented with literary forms other than poetry. In 1931 he began a novel, *Brother Death*, which includes characters who later reappeared in *Cry, the Beloved Country*, and in 1934 he wrote several chapters of a largely autobiographical novel, *John Henry Dane*; neither of these has been published. He also wrote a series of fragmentary stories, set in Ixopo, and one of them, "Secret for Seven," focuses on the cultural clash between whites and blacks that became one of his major themes. In addition he continued to produce poetry, and between 1932 and 1935 he wrote a play, *Louis Botha*, which showed his growing sympathies with the Afrikaners, whose language he was now learning. . . .

Reform School Warden

In 1934 he suffered a severe attack of enteric fever, from which he nearly died. The effects of this experience, combined with a renewed crisis in his marriage that prompted him to have an extramarital affair, made him determine on a change. He applied for the job of warden to each of the three reformatories in South Africa, hoping to get the job at the one in Cape Town; to his dismay, and the horror of his wife, he was appointed to South Africa's only reformatory for Africans, Diepkloof, outside Johannesburg. His friend Hofmeyr, who was now the minister of education, and thus had the final responsibility for reformatories, wrote to him that it was hard to know what could be done with the place. When Paton traveled up to take charge, in July 1935, he must have agreed with sinking heart.

Diepkloof had been built as a prison, and looked the part, with heavy bars on the windows, and with its grim, dilapidated buildings enclosed in a high barbed-wire fence. Uniformed guards, black and white, patrolled ceaselessly, armed with heavy sticks with which they administered beatings at will. The inmates, numbering about four hundred, ranged from boys of nine who had been confined for misdemeanors as small as stealing a single pot of jam, to young men in their early twenties who had committed rape or murder, and who would not hesitate to kill if need or opportunity arose. . . .

Paton came to think of Diepkloof as a microcosm of South African society. That such a comparison could be drawn in 1935 is a terrible indictment of South Africa fully thirteen years before the Nationalists came to power and shows how false is the view that apartheid dates from 1948. . . .

Paton came to think of Diepkloof's reform as a pattern for reforming South Africa as a whole. A semantic change, significantly enough, came first. Some months after Paton's arrival the Warden's title was changed to "Principal," the inmates were to be referred to henceforth as "pupils," the black head guard was to be the "Head Teacher," the other guards became "supervisors." The official name of the institution, in Afrikaans, became *Verbeteringskool*: "Reformatory School." Behind the semantic changes lay a conceptual alteration; Diepkloof had been transferred from the Department of Prisons to the Department of Education, and Paton was expected to transform the place, though his superiors admitted frankly that they had no idea what could be done with it.

Paton's answer was to introduce a series of rapid incremental changes, all designed to increase the freedom and the responsibility of the pupils. . . .

Attempts at Prison Reform

Above all he worked to integrate the Diepkloof inmates into the society of South Africa again, by building free hostels into which they could move after a time and live permanently outside the main block, and he planned, as a final step, to send them to a school inside the nearby black township, thereby linking them back into the society that had cast them out. His aim was nothing less than the healing of a riven society, and it was an aim that clearly had ramifications in the country as a whole.

Paton had not merely reformed Diepkloof, he had undergone a conversion himself, from the harsh disciplinarian he had been at Ixopo to a man who believed firmly in the superiority of love, or at any rate care, as an instrument of reformation and discipline. And he believed, increasingly, that it was a lesson the whole of South African society needed to learn. He tried hard to convert the education minister, Hofmeyr, to his point of view, in the hope that Hofmeyr would offer him a bigger job at his side in politics, but he was disappointed. In consequence he began to publicize his work at Diepkloof through frequent speeches and lectures, and, after 1942, he also began publishing a series of articles on the theory of prison reform and the value of liberal ideas. In several of these articles he put forward a comprehensive program for reforming South African society by bringing blacks into the mainstream of the nation's economic and political life.

His calls for action were on the whole ignored, however, by the general public as much as they had been by Hofmeyr, and there was one furious attack on him in 1945 by the editor of the influential Afrikaans newspaper *Die Transvaler* (Pretoria), Hendrik Frensch Verwoerd, who when the Nationalists came to power in 1948 became the chief architect of apartheid. Paton recognized that he was losing the war of ideas in South Africa; he needed to find a means of reaching the hearts of a wider audience.

Novel Is a Great Success

He found it during a tour he did in 1946–1947 of reformatories in Europe and North America. Traveling alone for months, inspecting reformatories by day and spending his nights in cheap hotels, Paton became intensely homesick and found himself thinking continuously of South Africa and his family. These longings, together with his reading of the works of John Steinbeck and Knut Hamsun, crystallized on 25 September 1946 in Norway, while he was sitting in the cathedral at Trondheim; he went back to his hotel room and began writing the novel he later titled *Cry, the Beloved Country*. He wrote it in hotels and on board ships, in Scandinavia, in England, in Canada, in the United States, and finished it in a hotel in San Francisco on 29 December 1946. The book was eventually published by Charles Scribner's Sons early in 1948. It was an immediate success, and its sales have continued to climb steadily, year by year: in 1991 just fewer than one hundred thousand copies of the novel were sold worldwide.

The reasons for this astonishingly sustained success are not hard to find. . . .

No bald summary can convey the extraordinary beauty of the language, or the deeply moving nature of the novel, with its plea for understanding and cooperation between the races. Its emotional drive is striking, and it is the chief thing the modern reader, particularly the non-South African reader, notices; however, the first readers of *Cry, the Beloved Country* saw it as a novel, not of emotion primarily, but of ideas, and they did not always like the ideas. . . .

Political Awareness

Cry, the Beloved Country is as much a didactic novel as anything Charles Dickens wrote. However, it is not just a didactic novel, and certainly it cannot be summed up as being "about" black-white conflicts; Paton was not a Marxist and this novel is not a work of socialist realism. It is a politically aware novel, however, and it has a definite political agenda behind it, a political agenda that had gradually became clear to Paton through his contact with young, delinquent blacks in his work as a reformatory warden. He believed that the system of separation of the races, by locking blacks out of any real possibility of advancement, was storing up disaster for his country, and he feared that by the time whites had come to recognize the wrong they were committing, it might be too late. "I have one great fear in my heart," says a black character in the most widely quoted passage from *Cry, the Beloved Country*, "that one day when they are turned to loving, they will find we are turned to hating."

The great success of *Cry, the Beloved Country*, which was accelerated by the coming to power of the National Party a few months after publication of the book, freed Paton from his work at Diepkloof; he resigned in April 1948 and devoted himself to writing full time. . . .

Late in 1951 he wrote another novel, working mostly in a London hotel; he called it *Too Late the Phalarope*, and it was the second of his novels to be published, in 1953. Whereas *Cry, the Beloved Country* had focused on the impact of South African society on blacks, *Too Late the Phalarope* places the Afrikaner at center stage, and in particular examines the effect on Afrikaner life of the laws against miscegenation, the Immorality Act and Mixed Marriages Act, which the Nationalist government had enacted. . . .

Founds the Liberal Party

In May 1953 he helped to found the South African Liberal Party, becoming one of its three vice presidents. He became its president a year later and retained that position until the party was forced to disband in 1968. The Liberal Party, though it never succeeded in getting one of its candidates elected to parliament, had influence well beyond its numbers, chiefly because of Paton's fame, and the fact that his was a voice that could not be silenced. During the 1960s and 1970s, when his colleagues, one after another, were banned and silenced, or chose to leave the country, Paton continued to speak out powerfully, in hundreds of articles and speeches, against the injustice and folly of apartheid. . . .

Throughout this period, however, Paton continued to spend time on more creative writing as well. He wrote the libretto for a musical set in a black township near Durban, with music by a black composer, Todd Matshikiza: the result, *Mkhumbane*, which opened in Durban just after the Sharpeville killings in March 1960, was a great success, and encouraged him to involve himself in another dramatic collaboration, *Sponono: A Play in Three Acts* (1965), which he wrote with [Indian director, producer, and screenwriter] Krishna Shah and which is based on three of Paton's short stories drawing on his Diepkloof years that were published in *Tales from a Troubled Land*. *Sponono* was such a success in South Africa in 1962 that it subsequently opened on Broadway in 1964 and has been revived several times since.

Paton also found time to write what he himself considered one of his best books, *Hofmeyr* (1964), a meticulously researched biography of his friend Hofmeyr, who had died in 1948. . . .

Hofmeyr is intended as more than just a tribute to a politician; it is a history of the Liberal movement in South Africa, and an examination of the apparent triumph of Afrikaner Nationalism—an examination, in other words, of how South Africa arrived at the desperate state it was in by 1964.

The study of recent South African history fascinated Paton all the more as the present grew more threatening. His passport was withdrawn by the government in 1960; shortly thereafter banning orders were issued against many Liberals, which prohibited them from attending or addressing meetings of any kind. Other Liberals were arrested; many fled abroad, and others turned to violence, calling themselves the African Resistance Movement (ARM) and blowing up power pylons during 1964. When the members of ARM were betrayed by one of their number and were arrested that same year, Paton, who had not known of their plans, felt profoundly wounded by their action; he himself became the focus of police harassment. He was deprived of his passport for a decade, he was threatened with house arrest, he was harassed and followed by police wherever he went, his telephone calls and mail were intercepted, his house was searched, and his car was first damaged and then destroyed, but he continued to warn and protest. His worldwide fame prevented the government from imprisoning him. The eventual outcome of this government campaign was the passing of a law in 1968 that made multiracial groups illegal, and rather than submit to it, the Liberal Party disbanded, a bitter blow to Paton.

Adjusts to Life's Changes

To add to the pressure on him at this time, his wife Dorrie, a lifelong smoker, developed emphysema and was slowly dying through the second half of the 1960s. When she died in October 1967, Paton himself wanted to die, and he went through a long period of demoralization and depression in which he left his mail unanswered and drank heavily. In a curious echo of *Too Late the Phalarope*, Paton received a great deal of adverse publicity when he was accused of trying to procure the sexual services of a black woman. This accusation was never proven, but neither was it refuted.

From this period of depression he was saved by his secretary, Anne Hopkins: they fell in love with one another during 1968 and married in January 1969. There were strains in the marriage, for Anne Hopkins was more than twenty years younger than Paton and had two teenage children of her own from a previous marriage; a good deal of adjustment was required on both sides. But Anne proved highly effective at protecting Paton from the multitude of calls on his time that frittered away his energies, and under her influence Paton began writing again.

His first major book after his remarriage was *Kontakion for You Departed*, also published in the United States as *For You Departed* (1969). It is a deeply moving account of Paton's first marriage, half memoir, half religious meditation on the meanings of life and death, and in it he made the first attempt to review his life, a review that he continued with distinction in his volumes of autobiography. . . .

Political Work Continues

The worst of the government pressure on himself and the Liberal Party had passed by the mid 1970s, but this was in part because the party was seen to be too weak to pose any threat to Nationalist rule. For the next decade the Liberal Party seemed ever more marginalized, ignored by most South African whites, contemptuously regarded as a fellow traveler of communism, and unable to get any of its candidates into Parliament. However, Paton continued to work tirelessly for the Party and to pour a great part of his annual income into party coffers. . . .

In 1977, at the age of seventy-four, Paton began summing up his life as a whole in a first volume of autobiography, *Towards the Mountain*, published in 1980. The title refers to that holy mountain of the Lord mentioned by Isaiah, where none shall hurt or destroy; and the volume was as much a vision of the ideal society as an account of Paton's own life. It takes his own story from birth up to the time he published *Cry, the Beloved Country*; but every detail is chosen, not just for the light it sheds on Alan Paton the individual, but for the light it sheds on the society in which he grew up, and for the indication it gives of the kind of society South Africa could become. This theme gives the book its remarkable unity; Paton looks before and after, and the book is as much a prophecy as a memoir.

In 1980, at the age of seventy-seven, he embarked on the second volume of his autobiography and found himself dealing with the period, during the 1950s and 1960s, of his greatest political involvement. He abandoned the project temporarily. It was at this point that he conceived the plan of writing the story, not in the form of a memoir, but as a trilogy of novels. The first of the projected series, *Ah, But Your Land Is Beautiful*, was written with great rapidity, and published in 1981. . . .

Ah, But Your Land Is Beautiful was received politely but without real enthusiasm by the critics. This lack of enthusiasm was partly because of the complexity of its plot and the large number of its characters, which reflected the difficulty Paton had experienced in trying to turn history into art; however, it was also because the simple, solemn power of *Cry, the Beloved Country* and even of *Too Late the Phalarope* was lacking in *Ah, But Your Land Is Beautiful*; the humane vision was obscured by a busy involvement in the details of South African politics, and even Paton's character sketches seemed constrained by his determination to do justice to the originals on whom he was drawing. . . .

In 1984 he began working once again on the second volume of his autobiography, *Journey Continued*, and finished it just before his death. It was posthumously published in 1988. The work is a less appealing volume than *Towards the Mountain*, for much of it consists of detailed history, the result of research rather than of memory transmuted through art. In the second half of it there is a sense of flaccidity and tiredness, which perhaps results from the fact that he was in his eightieth year by the time he returned to writing it.

He continued his wide range of activities until just before his death, continuing to travel with enjoyment, to serve on the editorial board of the Liberal journal *Contact*, to take an active part in such political gatherings as the Natal Indaba with the Zulus, and to turn out his newspaper articles. Alan Paton died 12 April 1988 after a short struggle with cancer of the esophagus, and his ashes were scattered in the beautiful garden of his

Botha's Hill home, in the cool hills not far from Pietermaritzburg, where his journey had begun eighty-five years before. . . .

His talent was multifaceted, displaying itself not just in novels, but in poetry, in two pioneering biographies, in his autobiographies, in his devotional volume *Instrument of Thy Peace*, and that remarkable book *Kontakion for You Departed*, which is a combination of the biographical and the devotional. The unparalleled success of *Cry, the Beloved Country*, paradoxically, obscured the richness of his other achievements, and it is likely that a mature assessment of his full value in the context of South African literature has yet to be made. His was a profoundly humane and civilized vision, and the apparent triumph in South Africa in the 1990s of the values for which he strove and wrote throughout his life, would have given him deep satisfaction had he lived to see it.

Racial Inequality Was a Central Theme in Paton's Life and Writings

Contemporary Authors Online

Contemporary Authors Online is a Web-based reference work featuring biographical sketches of modern authors.

The following excerpt describes how Alan Paton's commitment to racial equality in South Africa is reflected in his classic work, Cry, the Beloved Country, as well as in all the fiction and nonfiction that he wrote following it. In his later life, Paton was criticized for his opposition to sanctions against South Africa. However, his position was consistent with his lifelong beliefs, according to the author.

One of the earliest proponents of racial equality in his native South Africa, Alan Paton first came into the public eye in 1948 with his novel *Cry, the Beloved Country*. A landmark publication for its time, the novel follows the fate of a young black African, Absalom Kumalo, who, having murdered a white citizen, "cannot be judged justly without taking into account the environment that has partly shaped him," as Edmund Fuller writes in his book *Man in Modern Fiction: Some Minority Opinions on Contemporary American Writing*. The environment in question is typified by the hostility and squalid living conditions facing most of South Africa's nonwhites, victims of South Africa's system of apartheid. . . .

Laws Against Miscegenation

Paton followed *Cry, the Beloved Country* with another socially conscious novel, *Too Late the Phalarope*. This volume centers on a white Afrikaner, Pieter, whose youthful idealism has

Contemporary Authors Online, "Alan (Stewart) Paton," Farmington Hills, MI: The Gale Group, 2003. Copyright © 2003 by Thomson Gale. Reproduced by permission of Gale, a part of Cengage Learning.

tragic consequences. The story hinges on Pieter's love affair with a black girl; according to Alfred Kazin in the *New York Times Book Review*, "Under the 'Immorality Act' of the country, sexual relations between whites and blacks are a legal offense." As Kazin goes on to explain, "Pieter is sent to prison, his father strikes [the youth's] name from the great family Bible and dies of shame, and the whole family withdraws from the community in horror at Pieter's crime 'against the race.'"

"Invariably, comparisons [of *Too Late the Phalarope*] with *The Scarlet Letter* and *Crime and Punishment* arise," as Fuller points out in another work, *Books with Men behind Them*. "Once Pieter has committed his act, there is no possible release for him but total exposure—a dilemma he shares in part with [*The Scarlet Letter*'s] Arthur Dimmesdale and [*Crime and Punishment*'s] Raskolnikov. Paton gives us a long sequence of superb suspense, arising out of guilty misunderstandings of innocent natural coincidences. But just as the death wish is commonly unconscious, so Pieter suffers an agonized dread of discovery, unconscious of the fact that it is that exposure and its consequences that have motivated him from the start."

Highlights Injustices

A handful of nonfiction works and biographies followed Paton's second novel, but the author received more critical attention for his 1981 book, *Ah, But Your Land Is Beautiful*, which was his first novel in 28 years. The story opens with an act of quiet rebellion. An Indian teenager named Prem enters the Durban Library in Natal, South Africa, and sits down to read. Since she is not white, she is barred from using the facility. However, Prem defies the authorities, and her struggle ignites the embryonic anti-apartheid campaigns of the 1950s. The story goes on to trace the history of such organizations as the Liberal Party (of which Paton was president from 1958 to 1968).

As *Chicago Tribune Book World* reviewer Charles R. Larson sees it, the novel "fairly groans under the weight of human misery and havoc." He also states that "readers unfamiliar with the horrors of South African politics may be shocked to learn of apartheid legislation against racial mixing at every level of human contact—including funerals and religious services." "Paton's determination to expose injustice is so overwhelming that too often his characters have little life beyond their roles in his morality drama," John Rechy writes in a *Los Angeles Times Book Review* article. "Emphasizing their admirable hope and courage, he at times denies them the full, defining power of their rage. The unfortunate result is that the evil, too, becomes faceless; a disembodied voice of inquisition barking out injustice." But whatever artistic criticism he has for *Ah, But Your Land Is Beautiful*, Rechy concludes that he "respectfully [envies] Paton's courageous hopefulness, which has allowed him, at age 78 [at the time of publication] to continue to believe that justice may prevail in his beautiful land of entrenched evil." . . .

Two Autobiographies

Originally Paton had hoped to make *Ah, But Your Land Is Beautiful* the first part of a trilogy of novels about South African race relations. Weakened by a heart condition, however, he concentrated on his autobiography. He finished the first volume, *Towards the Mountain*, in 1980, and the second, *Journey Continued*, just before his death in 1988. The books describe Paton's early years as an educator, when he observed the social inequities that prompted *Cry, The Beloved Country*, and his later involvement with the Liberal party, which dissolved in 1968 rather than purge its nonwhite members as the government demanded. In his last years Paton was criticized by many anti-apartheid activists because he opposed their efforts to pressure the government by discouraging foreign investment in South Africa. Such sanctions, Paton argued, would unduly punish South Africa's poorest blacks, and he decried even Nobel Prize–winning clergyman Desmond Tutu for supporting such a strategy. Though controversial, Paton saw his actions as consistent with a lifelong belief in progress through moderation and mutual understanding. As he wrote in *Journey Continued*: "By liberalism I don't mean the creed of any party or any century. I mean a generosity of spirit, a tolerance of others, an attempt to comprehend otherness, a commitment to the rule of law, a high ideal of the worth and dignity of man, a repugnance for authoritarianism and a love of freedom."

Paton Drew on His Faith and Experience to Write *Cry, the Beloved Country*

Lewis Gannett

Lewis Gannett was a journalist, book critic, and author of several books on travel and literature, including John Steinbeck. *For many years he wrote a column called* Books and Things *for the* New York Herald Tribune.

The following selection is an introduction to Cry, the Beloved Country, *in which Lewis Gannett calls the book both "passionately African" and "universal." Stating that the book came from Alan Paton's life experiences, Gannett finds reflections from Paton's work as the principal of a reform school. Gannett quotes Paton extensively in his introduction, ending with Paton's belief that only love can conquer fear.*

C*ry, the Beloved Country* may be longer remembered than any other novel of 1948, but not because it fits into any pattern of the modern novel. It stands by itself; it creates rather than follows a tradition. It is at once unashamedly innocent and subtly sophisticated. It is a story; it is a prophecy; it is a psalm. It is passionately African, as no book before it had been; it is universal. It has in it elements of autobiography; yet it is selfless.

Life as Preparation

Let the reader discover the story for himself. Alan Paton tells something of its pre-publication history in his own author's introduction. The rest is still living history. In the United

States, where it first saw print, the book had a small advance sale—3300 copies. It had no book-club fanfare in advance of publication; it never reached the top of the bestseller lists. But it made its way. People discovered it for themselves. They are still discovering it.

In South Africa it had a fantastic success. In that country of barely two million whites and nearly ten million mostly illiterate blacks, its present sale of thirty-odd thousand copies is the equivalent of a sale of more than two million copies in the United States. No other book in South African history ever stirred such an overwhelming response—and the aftermath of this response in the South African conscience is still to be written.

Alan Paton himself is a native son of South Africa, born in Pietermaritzburg in the east coast province of Natal in 1903. His father, a Scots Presbyterian and something of a poet, went out to South Africa as a civil servant just before the Boer War; his mother, though of English stock, was a third-generation South African. Alan Paton's entire schooling was South African. At college in Pietermaritzburg, he specialized in science and in off hours he wrote poetry. Until the European-American trip on which *Cry, the Beloved Country* came spilling out of his subconsciousness, he had been out of South Africa only once—at twenty-one, when he attended an Empire Students Conference in London, and followed that with a motorcycle trip through England and Scotland.

Just out of college, he wrote two novels—and almost immediately destroyed the manuscripts. He wrote some poetry. In his middle years he wrote serious essays—much such essays as Arthur Jarvis writes in the novel—for liberal South African magazines. It was life, rather than literature, which prepared Paton to write *Cry, the Beloved Country*.

Transforms More than a Reform School

After college Alan Paton taught in good schools—schools established for the sons of the rich, white minority in South Africa. One of them was in Ixopo (in Natal), in those grass-covered hills lovely beyond any singing of it, where the titihoya, the bird of the veld, sings in his book. It was there that he met Dorrie Francis, the girl he married, the mother of his two South-African schooled sons. She is also a born South African. Then he went to teach in Pietermaritzburg, and there, when he was about thirty, he suffered a severe attack of enteric fever. His illness gave him time to think. He did not, he decided, want to make a life career of teaching the sons of the rich.

South Africa was in one of its periods of fermenting change in 1934. One of the new reforms transferred all correctional institutions for young people under twenty-one from the Ministry of Justice to the Ministry of Education, and the Minister of Education at that time was one of South Africa's great men, Jan Hofmeyr. Had he lived, Hofmeyr might have succeeded to General Smuts' mantle (he became Deputy Prime Minister in 1939) and perhaps have changed the recent course of South African history. A Boer who dared to tell his fellow Afrikaners that they must give up "thinking with the blood," must "maintain the essential value of human personality as something independent of race or color," must supplant fear with faith, Hofmeyr was one of Alan Pawn's heroes; as a boy Paton had gone camping with him. Later, the South African edition of *Cry, the Beloved Country* was dedicated to Jan Hofmeyr; it appeared three months before Hofmeyr's death. And the only poem which Alan Paton has published since his college days was a poem on the death of Hofmeyr.

So, recovering from his fever, Alan Paton wrote to Hofmeyr asking for a job. Somewhat to his horror, he got it—as principal of Diepkloof Reformatory, a huge prison school for delinquent black boys, set up in a sort of barbed-wire stockade on the edge of South Africa's greatest city, Johannesburg. It was a penitentiary, a place of locked cells and of despair. In ten years, under Hofmeyr's inspiring leadership, Alan Paton transformed the place. The barbed-wire vanished and gardens of geraniums took its place; the bars were torn down; the whole atmosphere changed. Some of these boys made good; and some, like Absalom in *Cry, the Beloved Country*, did not. You will find suggestions of Diepkloof in Alan Paton's novel, and there is a little of Paton himself in the anonymous young white man at the school, as well as in the character of Arthur Jarvis.

The "experiment" lasted more than ten years, a fertile interval, though Paton himself calls it a "period of aridity" in his literary life. He wrote serious articles but no poetry or fiction. Out of the experiment grew Paton's prison-study trip to Scandinavia, England and America which bore such unexpected fruit in *Cry, the Beloved Country*. Paton felt so profoundly that he needed a change that he sold his life insurance policies to finance the trip away from Africa.

Written During His Travels

In Sweden Paton read and was moved by John Steinbeck's *Grapes of Wrath*. Possibly the reading of that novel turned his mind back to his earlier interest in creative writing. He had at first no plan to write a novel of his own. But, not speaking Swedish, he passed many nights alone in his hotel; and, as in his bout with enteric fever, he had time to think and wonder. One dark afternoon a friendly stranger took him to see the rose window in the cathedral of Trondheim by torchlight. That somberly glowing experience set the mood. Paton returned to his hotel, sat down at a desk and between five and seven, the whole first chapter of his novel poured out. He did not yet know what the rest of the story was to be. The theme was clear—he had been living it. The story seemed to form itself as he travelled. Parts were written in Stockholm, Trondheim, Oslo, London, and all the way across the United States; it was finished in San Francisco.

Then Paton went home to South Africa, and the book followed him, and changed his life. . . .

When Alan Paton flew to New York, in October, 1949; to see *Lost in the Stars*, the musical play Maxwell Anderson wrote upon themes from *Cry, the Beloved Country*, he spoke to a Book and Author luncheon upon the South African background of his novel. It was an eloquent and revealing profession of faith. To attempt to condense or paraphrase it would be foolish, so, with a few modifications made with Mr. Paton's consent, I quote it at length.

South Africa's Diverse Population

"I was born," he said, "in that country known as the Union of South Africa. The heart of it is a great interior plateau that falls on all sides to the sea. But when one thinks of it and remembers it, one is aware not only of mountains and valleys, not only of the wide rolling stretches of the veld, but of solemn and deep undertones that have nothing to do with any mountain or any valley, but have to do with men. By some these are but vaguely heard and dimly understood; but for others they are never silent, they become ever more obtrusive and dominant, till the stretch of the sky and veld is nothing more than the backdrop against which is being played a great human drama in which I am deeply involved, my wife and my children, all men and their wives and children, of all colors and tongues, in which all Africa is involved, and all humanity and the world. For no country is now an island, of itself entire.

"There are eleven to twelve million people in the Union of South Africa. Of these only two and one-half million are white, three-fifths of these being Afrikaans-speaking, two-fifths English-speaking. There are one million of what we call 'colored' people, the descendants of the racial mixture which took place before white custom and law hardened against it, and forbade it, under the influence of the white man's intense determination to survive on a black continent. There are about one-quarter million Indians, whose forefathers were brought out by the English settlers to work on the sugar farms of Natal. And there are eight million black people, the people of the African tribes.

Clash of Dutch and Native Cultures

The Afrikaans-speaking people are the descendants of the Dutch who first came to the Cape of Good Hope, which Francis Drake, the navigator, described as the fairest cape in all the circumference of the earth. These people did not come to Africa to settle, but the fertile valleys and great mountains of the Cape bound them with a spell.

"The primitive Bushmen and Hottentots could not stand up against this new thing that came out of Europe, and they melted away. But under the influence of the isolation of these vast spaces, and the hardships and loneliness of this patriarchal life, the people from Europe and the language from Holland changed. Something African entered into both people and language, and changed them. This the people themselves recognized and they called themselves the Afrikaners. Their new and simple and flexible and beautiful language they called Afrikaans; their love of this new country was profound and passionate.

"But still another change awaited them. As the Afrikaners moved yet further north they encountered the warlike tribes of the black African people. A long and bloody warfare ensued between them. The black men were numerous and savage and determined; the history of this encounter is one of terror and violence. The black people became truly a part of the white man's mind.

"Under the influence of this danger, the Afrikaner attitude toward black men hardened. The safety and survival of the small band of white people were seen as dependent on the rigid separation of white and black. It became the law that the

Armed Zulus dance at a gathering on December 16, 1998, at Blood River near Vryheid, South Africa. Thousands of Zulus marked the slaughter of 3000 of their forebears by Boer settlers in the 1838 Battle of Blood River that became a mythical underpinning of apartheid. AP Images.

relationship between white and black was to be that between master and servant; and it became the iron law that between white men and black women, between black men and white women, there was to be no other relationship but this. Land was set aside for the conquered tribes, but, as we see so clearly today, never enough.

The English Arrive

"Yet another powerful influence entered into the making of the Afrikaner soul. In 1800 the English came to the Cape, during the Napoleonic Wars. They came initially, not as settlers, but as governors, officials, missionaries, teachers, traders, and fortune-seekers. Their attitude to the black man was different from that of the Afrikaner. The black man was not their enemy; he was their business. This fundamental incompatibility between two policies was to influence South African history for many years. It reached a climactic point in 1836, when many of the Afrikaner trekkers, abandoning all that they had so far gained, set out on the greatest trek of all, into the heart of the sub-continent, in order to escape the new and alien culture. There they set up the republics of the Transvaal and the Orange Free State. The position now was that the coastal regions of South Africa were English; the great interior plateau was Afrikaner; and on the fringes of both English and Afrikaner worlds lived the black men, doing the white man's work for him, steadily losing the dignity of their old ways of life.

"A new dramatic factor then entered the picture. In the interior of South Africa, in the very heart of the country to which the Afrikaner trekkers had gone to escape British rule, the richest gold of the world was discovered. The great modern, vigorous city of Johannesburg was born in a collection of tents and huts. Gold-seekers, many of them British, poured into the Transvaal. The Afrikaners watched with fear and anger and despair this new intrusion of the old enemy. The newcomers wanted the franchise; the Afrikaners dared not give it to them. And so a second great climax arrived, the Anglo-Boer War in 1899. The century-long incompatibility of a pastoral, agricultural, conservative community and a commercial, industrial, 'progressive' community exploded in war.

"In 1902 the Afrikaners capitulated. The British conscience, which was not to permit the British Crown ever again to engage in such a war, achieved the magnanimous settlement of 1906, by which self-government was restored to the defeated republics. A great wave of goodwill spread throughout the country, and four years later the Cape of Good Hope, the Orange Free State, the Transvaal and Natal came together to form the Union of South Africa, under the leadership of three defeated Afrikaner generals, General Botha, General Smuts and General Hertzog.

"But reconciliation was not so easily achieved. War, even when it is followed by magnanimity, leaves wounds not so easily healed. Twenty thousand Afrikaner women and children had died in the camps set up for their reception, mostly of typhoid fever. This was not easily forgotten. More important, the Afrikaner still feared that he and his world would be swallowed up and lost in the great British culture. He also saw a danger that the traditional English policy of laissez-faire toward the black people might lead to his engulfment.

Afrikaner Nationalism

"So the Afrikaner again set about to re-establish his separateness and distinctness. He established cultural societies for the protection of his customs, history and language. And he succeeded magnificently, largely because of his fiery independent spirit, and also because the ballot box had been put into his hands by his British enemy. Thus emerged what is today known as Afrikaner nationalism, the persistent and implacable urge that eventually, in 1948, defeated General Smuts, to the astonishment of every part of the civilized world.

"In the meantime the position of the black people had been changing beyond recognition. The cities of Johannesburg, Cape Town and Durban boomed; inevitably they attracted from the impoverished native reserves a never-ending stream of black people seeking work and city lights. They saw and envied the white man's world—his wealth, his comfort and his alien ways; meanwhile their own ancient tribal controls had been weakening. Their young men went astray; their old men were troubled and puzzled. Crime increased; the racial character deteriorated in the wretched hovels where the black men huddled in the slums of the white man's cities. This is the central theme of my novel, *Cry, the Beloved Country.*

"As the black men began to pour into the cities, the white people of South Africa became more and more reminded of the dangers of engulfment. This was one of the great reasons why white South Africans put the Nationalists in power. Afraid of the possible consequences of the laissez-faire policy of the Smuts government, they voted in favor of a party that advocated stern control and strict separation of the races as the 'only solution' of South Africa's ever more complicated and difficult problems.

"So South Africa returned, for the time at least, to the old policy of 'survival and separation.' It is the white settler on a black continent, aware of his precariousness of tenure, who speaks today through the mouthpiece of the Malan government.

"But one must not imagine that this white settler is motivated solely by fear. He too, is a human creature. He has not lived upon the earth without being influenced by the great human ideas, notably by the ideas of Christianity. Therefore, he too is a divided creature, torn between his fears for his own safety and his desire for his own survival on the one hand, and on the other, by those ideas of justice and love which are at the very heart of his religion. We are witnessing today a struggle in the hearts of men, white men, between the claims of justice and of survival, of conscience and of fear.

Love Can Conquer Fear

"It is my own belief that the only power which can resist the power of fear is the power of love. It's a weak thing and a tender thing; men despise and deride it. But I look for the day when in South Africa we shall realize that the only lasting and worth-while solution of our grave and profound problems lies not in the use of power, but in that understanding and compassion without which human life is an intolerable bondage, condemning us all to an existence of violence, misery and fear."

Such is the beloved country of Alan Paton's faith, of his compassion, and his hope. In his novel, the music of its cry is a strangely blended folksong, with elements of Zulu and Xosa speech, and echoes of the rhythm of that Jewish-Christian

Bible which speaks with such peculiar intimacy to black men in both America and South Africa. In *Cry, the Beloved Country* it sings with a new-old beauty to the whole world, with a faith that the dawn which brings light to the mountain-tops will also bring light to the valleys—a shining faith which is of the essence of the novel.

Cry, the Beloved Country stands alone. We have had many novels from statesmen and reformers, almost all bad; many novels from poets, almost all thin. In Alan Paton's *Cry, the Beloved Country* the statesman, the poet and the novelist meet in a unique harmony.

Paton Challenged Racism in His Writing and Politics

Jonathan Paton

Jonathan Paton, a son of Alan Paton, was a writer and the author of The Land and People of South Africa.

Jonathan Paton provides a very personal, subjective assessment of his father's life and work in the following viewpoint. He suggests that his father modeled the character Arthur Jarvis after himself and used Jarvis as a spokesperson for his own views on race relations. According to Jonathan Paton, the two themes of Cry, the Beloved Country *are detribalization and fear. However, his father, a devout Christian, believed that love could conquer fear and restore harmony between races.*

It is not easy for the son to write a critical appreciation of his father's books. It would be far easier for me to write an autobiography entitled "Son of Alan Paton," in which I would spell out both humorously and seriously the advantages and disadvantages of being the son of the great South African writer. Let me add that the disadvantages far outweigh the advantages. In this essay, I have resisted the temptation to speak of "my father" and will instead refer to him as "Alan Paton" or "Paton." However, I shall continue to write the essay in the first person, and in my comments on the various works the reader will detect a subjective, personal approach, not a detached analytical and critical style.

Cry, the Beloved Country was Alan Paton's first published novel. He had published several poems in student magazines

Jonathan Paton, "Alan Paton: Comfort in Desolation," *International Literature in English: Essays on the Major Writers*, edited by Robert L. Ross, Danvers, MA: Garland Publishing, 1991, pp. 161–67. Copyright © 1991 Robert L. Ross. All rights reserved. Republished with permission of Garland Publishing, conveyed through Copyright Clearance Center, Inc.

in his youth and had attempted and abandoned at least two novels in the 1920s and early 1930s, but he did not earn the reputation of a "writer" until the publication of *Cry, the Beloved County*. This novel gripped the imagination of the world and became a best seller overnight. In New York, Maxwell Anderson and Kurt Weill turned it into a successful musical, *Lost in the Stars*, which opened on Broadway in 1949. Soon afterward London Films produced a film of the novel, directed by Zolton Korda. Some readers in the United States and Great Britain were familiar with the works of South African poets and writers like Roy Campbell, William Plomer, and Olive Schreiner before the Second World War, but there is no doubt, as a South African critic once remarked, that *Cry, the Beloved Country* placed South Africa firmly on the international literary map.

In the introduction to *Cry, the Beloved County* Paton explains that although the novel is fictitious, it is largely rooted in fact—most of the events are fictional but certain events are "a compound of truth and fiction." "In these respects therefore," he writes, "the story is not true, but considered as a social record it is the plain and simple truth." Moral considerations are also important to Paton, considerations based on his Christian beliefs, even though throughout his career he was opposed to literature that was essentially didactic. Nevertheless he once stated that his aim was to write books that would "stab South Africa in the conscience." I believe that apart from narrating a gripping story, Paton is deliberately attempting to do just that in the pages of *Cry, the Beloved Country*.

Paton wrote the novel while he was away from South Africa, touring Scandinavia, Britain, and the United States, visiting reformatories and other penal institutions—he was still principal of Diepkloof Reformatory. He began the book in a lonely hotel room in Trondheim, Norway, and finished it in San Francisco. This was Paton's first lengthy visit away from his native land, and he was filled with nostalgia for his beloved country. While visiting the cathedral in Trondheim, he was deeply moved by the beauty of a large rose window. He left the cathedral filled with "strange emotions," returned to his hotel room and wrote down, almost without hesitation: "There is a lovely road that runs from Ixopo into the hills" and then completed the rest of the chapter before going out to dinner. Ixopo is a beautiful country village in Natal where Paton had met and fallen in love with his first wife, Dorrie. At the same time he had also fallen in love with the extraordinary beauty of Ixopo's rolling hills covered in grass and bracken, "lovely beyond any singing of it."

While strong feelings of nostalgia drove Paton to begin writing *Cry, the Beloved Country*, he certainly did not write a nostalgic novel. The story of the simple Zulu parson, Stephen Kumalo, and his desperate search for his son, Absalom, in the vast city of Johannesburg, arouses a wide range of emotions. The novel is indeed, as it is subtitled, "a stow of comfort in desolation." It is also a story of the injustices of segregation and the white man's laws. Readers will notice I have not used the word "apartheid." Paton wrote the novel toward the end of 1946. It was only in 1948 (the year of the novel's publication) that the Afrikaner Nationalist government came into power and entrenched "apartheid." The injustices, however, of the system go back a long way, for it was in the nineteenth century that the blacks lost most of their land. By 1946 Paton had been principal of Diepkloof Reformatory for eleven years, and he had discovered the appalling consequences of migratory labor. Black men were attracted to places like Johannesburg to work in the mines and other industries, but their wives and children were not allowed to accompany them. The character of Arthur Jarvis in the novel is very much modeled on Paton himself. After Jarvis is murdered, his father spends some time in his son's study reading from a manuscript that is still incomplete. Here is one of the passages he reads:

It was permissible when we discovered gold to bring labour to the mines. It was permissible to build compounds and to keep women and children away from the towns. It was permissible as an experiment, in the light of what we knew. But in the light of what we know now, with certain exceptions, it is no longer permissible. It is not permissible for us to go on destroying family life when we know that we are destroying it.

These views were very much Paton's own and were to lead him into a head-on clash with the Afrikaner Nationalist government in later years.

A great deal has been written about the style of *Cry, the Beloved Country*, so not much will be said about it here. The language on the whole is simple, yet profound. There are many cadences that bring to mind passages from the King James version of the Bible. Paton was a devout Christian and read and reread the Bible many times. He was also familiar with the Zulu language, and on occasion the prose imitates the style of Zulu speech rhythms. Of course, there are several other styles in the book, one of which is illustrated in the example of Arthur Jarvis's forceful indictment of migrant labor. This is often the style used by Paton in his nonfictional writing.

The central theme of the novel is, in my opinion, the theme of detribalization, of social disintegration. Before the industrial revolution began in South Africa, most black people lived in the tribal homelands, areas that had been allocated to them after they were dispossessed of most of their land. But the stretches where they lived were on the whole of poor quality, partly due to the nature of the terrain, partly due to overgrazing and ignorance of conservation methods. Paton describes that land vividly in *Cry, the Beloved Country*:

The great red hills stand desolate, and the earth has torn away like flesh. . . . Down in the valleys women scratch the soil that is left, and the maize hardly reaches the height of a man. They are valleys of old men and old women, of mothers and children. The men are away, the young men and the girls are away. The soil cannot keep them anymore.

The men and the women could no longer support their families and moved to the cities. Some sent money and returned home once a year to visit; but others neglected their families and found lovers. The stories of Absalom and of Gertrude and of John Kumalo are the stories of thousands upon thousands of black South Africans even today. As principal of Diepkloof Reformatory, Paton made a close study of juvenile crime in the cities and found that the root causes were the breakup of family life and the lack of a tribal support system. Overcrowded slums and unemployment contributed further to the growing crime wave.

Another theme that runs through the novel is the theme of fear, for there is fear throughout the land. At the beginning, Kumalo is afraid to open the letter from Johannesburg. He is afraid of Johannesburg. He is afraid that when people go to Johannesburg they do not come back. Later in the novel, Msimangu tells Kumalo: "It is fear that rules this land." Whites fear that blacks will rob them of their land and possessions. Blacks fear the cruelty of the white man's law. The author's voice also takes up this theme:

> Cry, the beloved country, for the unborn child that is the inheritor of our fear. . . . Let him not be moved when the birds of the land are singing, nor give too much of his heart to a mountain or a valley. For fear will rob him of all if he gives too much.

But the most striking illustration of the theme of fear is the remark that Msimangu makes to Kumalo about white people: "I have one great fear in my heart, that one day when they are turned to loving, they will find we are turned to hating." It is remarkable to think that Paton wrote these words in 1946. In the late 1980s the Afrikaner Nationalist government began to redress some of the wrongs of the past, but many black leaders claimed that it was doing "too little, too late." In fairness, however, it should be pointed out that in 1990 there are hundreds of thousands of black people who *do not* hate whites and who *do* seek reconciliation.

It would be wrong to conclude these comments about *Cry, the Beloved Country* on a note of destruction and fear. It is, after all, a story of *comfort* in desolation. In *Alan Paton*, Edward Callan points out the counter-theme of the need to restore: "Stephen Kumalo's physical search for his son, Absalom, and James Jarvis's intellectual search for his son, Arthur" both resulted in "an inner, spiritual awakening." The reader cannot fail to see the author's optimism in the belief that restoration will follow disintegration. And the theme of fear is counterbalanced by the theme of love, rooted in Paton's Christian convictions. Until his death in 1988, he refused to give up the struggle for racial reconciliation in South Africa. For he *did* believe that one day the dawn would come "of our emancipation, from the fear of bondage and the bondage of fear."

I have devoted a considerable portion of this essay to a discussion of *Cry, the Beloved Country*, partly because it is by far the best known of Paton's works, but also because I believe it is essential reading if one is to understand the complex issues that exist in South Africa in 1990. Certain sections of the novel have become dated, but most of it remains relevant forty years later.

Paton on more than one occasion remarked that his second novel, *Too Late the Phalarope*, was a better novel than *Cry, the Beloved Country*. However, he did not go into great detail on his reasons. All he would say is that *Too Late the Phalarope* had a "better structure." I would agree with this view, but at the same time I think I can understand why the work never enjoyed the popularity of the first novel, particularly outside South Africa. One reason lies in the title of the book. The phalarope (pronounced "fallarope") is a bird found in several parts of the world, including South Africa and the

United States. But it is rarely seen and is totally unknown to most people. I have met many people who have heard of the book, but who have not the slightest idea of what a phalarope is, let alone how the strange word is pronounced. . . .

After *Too Late the Phalarope* Paton ceased writing novels for some time. He continued to write short stories, poems, political articles, religious works, two biographies, and two volumes of his own autobiography. I wish to comment briefly on his third and last novel, *Ah, But Your Land Is Beautiful*, appearing nearly 30 years after *Too Late the Phalarope*. In the 1970s Paton had read and found most impressive Paul Scott's *The Raj Quartet*. The mixture of fact and fiction in these four novels intrigued Paton. Around 1980 he decided that he would attempt to depict South Africa's contemporary history as Scott had done with India. He planned a trilogy: the first novel would be based on the decade of the 1950s, the second on the 1960s, the third on the 1970s, including the riots in Soweto in 1976.

Ah, But Your Land Is Beautiful, set in the 1950s, is not, in my opinion, a success. It lacks the deeply moving qualities of *Cry, the Beloved Country* as well as its compassion and messages of comfort in desolation. While it is also an indictment of racial discrimination, there is no character in the novel whose personal tragedy is depicted so vividly and terrifyingly as that of Stephen Kumalo or Pieter van Vlaanderen. The characters, on the whole, are much shallower than the characters of the earlier novels. Mansfield, the white liberal, is clearly based to some extent on the author himself. Actual historical personages such as Trevor Huddleston and Albert Lutuli also appear in the novel. I think that Paton realized he had lost the art of novel writing (while still remaining a superb writer), for he abandoned the rest of the trilogy.

Paton is so well known as the author of *Cry, the Beloved Country* that many readers are unaware that he also wrote several excellent short stories. In 1960 some of these were published in New York under the title *Tales from a Troubled Land* and in London as *Debbie Go Home*. Most of these stories are based on his experiences at Diepkloof Reformatory and are accounts of sometimes tragic, sometimes comic episodes involving inmates and staff of the reformatory. Perhaps the best of these is "Sponono," a story in which the principal and an incorrigible inmate are involved in a seemingly endless duel about the nature of forgiveness. This story was turned into a musical and enjoyed a reasonably successful run on Broadway in 1964. Paton's best story is, in my opinion, "The Hero of Currie Road," published in the collection *Knocking on the Door*. It is a story, told with pathos and humor, of the dilemma that confronts a white South African liberal in his attempts to fight against white racism on one hand and militant black nationalism, which condones violence, on the other. It is again, to some extent, the story of Paton's own life.

The bulk of Paton's writing, which will not be discussed here, falls under the heading of nonfiction. The author became increasingly interested in the writing of biography and devoted many years of his life to the researching and writing of the biography entitled *Hofmeyr*. Jan Hofmeyr, one of South Africa's most brilliant sons, was a close friend of Paton's, and his strongly held liberal beliefs exerted a powerful influence on the author. Paton's biography tells of Hofmeyr's domination by his mother and by General Jan Smuts, South Africa's Prime Minister during the 1940s. Hofmeyr could never break free of Smuts's domination and failed in his attempts to steer South Africa in a more liberal direction; hence the American edition of this book was entitled *South African Tragedy*. Paton's second biography, less intriguing than *Hofmeyr*, was entitled *Apartheid and the Archbishop*, and is about a former Archbishop of Cape Town, Geoffrey Clayton.

For me, Paton's most moving work is *Kontakion for You Departed*, which narrates the story of the author's life with his wife Dorrie. It is an account of my mother and father's life together, and I was moved to tears when I first read it. I find it extremely painful to reread. (In the United States the book is called *For You Departed*.)

In conclusion, I shall mention briefly the two parts of Paton's autobiography. The first is called *Towards the Mountain* and tells in remarkably frank detail the story of the author's life from 1903 to 1948. The second, *Journey Continued*, is far less frank and, I think, considerably less successful. But I do find its conclusion very moving, written as it was shortly before Alan Paton's death. I should like to end by quoting the concluding lines:

> I shall not write anything more of any weight. I am grateful that life made it possible for me to pursue my writing career. I am now ready to go when I am called.
>
> God bless Africa
>
> Guard her children
>
> Guide her rulers
>
> And give her peace
>
> Amen.

Paton Created a Classic

Dan Jacobson

Dan Jacobson is a novelist, short story writer, critic, essayist, and professor. Born in South Africa, he published several novels with South African themes, including The Trap.

The following memoir was delivered by Dan Jacobson at a memorial service for Alan Paton. Jacobson's special interest in Paton stems from an intense lecture on race relations that Paton delivered to Jacobson's high school. Jacobson acknowledges the dismissal of Paton's talent at the time of his death—quoting a review that refers to Cry, the Beloved Country *as a "South African Uncle Tom's Cabin." He turns this criticism to a compliment, however, saying that both novels are "proverbial"—becoming part of a common stock of reference.*

Forty-three years ago Alan Paton came to my home town, Kimberley, to make an oration and to give away the prizes at the annual speech-day of the school I attended, the Kimberley Boys' High School. This was well before he had become a household name in South Africa and a familiar one in many countries outside it. He was invited, as far as I can recall, because he had been an acquaintance of our headmaster's, when they had been students together at Rhodes University. All we were told about our guest's public life before-hand was that he was the principal of the reformatory for young black offenders at Diepkloof, near Johannesburg.

A Memorable Speech

The ceremony took place not in the school itself, but amid the creaking floors, lofty windows, and forlornly distempered walls of Kimberley's old Town Hall. Alan Paton duly gave out

Dan Jacobson, "Nostalgia for the Future," *Times Literary Supplement*, July 29–August 4, 1988, p. 830. Copyright © 1988 by The Times Supplements Limited. Reproduced from *Times Literary Supplement* by permission.

the prizes; among many others, I had the privilege of going up to receive a book or two, a handshake, a rather stern glance, and a few muttered words of congratulation. Then, that part of the proceedings over, we settled down to listen to what I and my schoolfriends expected to be the usual speech-day affair: one which would be congratulatory, patronizing, full of references to the sterling work of our teachers and our own achievements on the sports field.

We did not get such a speech. We got instead an intense, almost angry-sounding lecture about the injustices of the social and racial conditions prevailing in South Africa and the dangers which confronted the country as a result—and about the ways in which we might try to meet those dangers. I can remember vividly how slight the speaker's figure appeared to be, in his double-breasted suit, and how earnest was his manner; how his brow gleamed under the lights on that warm Kimberley evening; and, above all, how unlike anything we had heard before at any school occasion was what he was saying to us. Whether our headmaster—not an enlightened man, in any sense—was pleased with his guest's performance, I cannot tell; some of the boys, I know, did not like it. But all of us were aware that every word addressed to us had been said out of conviction, out of a sense of imperative need.

A Lasting Book

That was to be my sole meeting with Alan Paton; the contact he and I were to have subsequently, decades later, was to be by correspondence only. *Cry, the Beloved Country* came out just a few years after his visit to Kimberley, when I was a student at Witwatersrand University. Naturally, I felt a special interest in the book, because of my recollection of the occasion I have described; in any case novels about South Africa were much rarer then than they are now. I was moved by the book, and I heard clearly in it the fierce cadences of the voice that had addressed us that night in Kimberley. But I had literary and critical misgivings about the book too—about its homiletic tone, especially, and about the incorporation in it of relatively straightforward passages of contemporary history. So when I read, in a short-lived student publication, a review in which it was cuttingly described as "the South African *Uncle Tom's Cabin*", I at once recognized—or thought I recognized—what the writer meant. This was all the easier for me to do since at that time I had not actually read *Uncle Tom's Cabin*.

And today? The description still seems to me in some ways just; but it also seems to me a more honourable one than I would ever have supposed then. There are certain novels, of a relatively rare kind, which cannot be adequately assessed in literary terms—though they obviously use literary and imaginative means to achieve their effects. Nor can such novels be described solely in the language of politics—though their intentions are always and avowedly political. Nor is the power they have wholly to be identified with the fervour of the moral homilies they contain. Rather, precisely because they have no regard for the very distinctions I have just tried to make between the literary, the political, and the moral, such works sometimes acquire a life in the minds of readers that may best be described as *proverbial*. Even for non-readers, they become part of a common stock of reference and of modes of self-recognition. *Uncle Tom's Cabin* was such a book; so (to take a very different example) was Orwell's *Nineteen Eighty-four*; so too, for countless numbers of South Africans, and people elsewhere, was *Cry, the Beloved Country*. Books like these endure long beyond the particular conditions that produce them; and they do so because they themselves have become one of the factors governing the self-consciousness of the communities to which they are addressed.

None of Alan Paton's other writings achieved the success of *Cry, the Beloved Country*; about a success of that order one is tempted to say that lightning never strikes twice in the same place. Among his later works, though, I do want to mention the biography of Jan Hofmeyr, a book which was bound to rouse a peculiar nostalgia in someone of my own generation, and which evidently roused a rather more painful nostalgia in its author. Jan Hofmeyr, Jan Smuts's lieutenant and, it was supposed, the man who would be his successor, was always thought of as the flag-bearer of a native, Afrikaner liberalism. His unfulfilled career has therefore remained one of the most tantalizing might-have-beens of South African public and political life. However, the nostalgia informing Alan Paton's biography was not only for the past, but also—and this is what made it so painful—for the future, for the possible and impossible country of which the author had always dreamed: a South Africa which would find in the varieties of its peoples a cause for celebration rather than despair.

Social Issues in Literature

CHAPTER 2

Cry, the Beloved Country and Race Relations

Cry, the Beloved Country Is One of the Best Books of Our Time

James Stern

James Stern was a novelist and short story writer whose work includes The Heartless Land.

In this early review of Cry, the Beloved Country, *James Stern finds it one of the most beautifully written and best books of the time. Stern notes that Alan Paton has drawn a heartbreaking portrait of suffering and dignity in the Reverend Stephen Kumalo and predicts that Kumalo will be a lasting figure in literature.*

Many good books have come out of South Africa, and no doubt many more will come, but it is difficult to believe that any will compare favorably with Alan Paton's *Cry, the Beloved Country*. Since Olive Schreiner's *The Story of a South African Farm* (1883), colonial literature has produced nothing like it, so far as I know. To say that Paton's is the more profound, compassionate, dramatic and important book is probably to say that *Cry, the Beloved Country* is one of the best novels of our time. In the magic, symbolic Zulu idiom of its prose, it is without doubt one of the most beautifully written.

Rings with Compassion

In such praise I believe Olive Schreiner would surely join. One can imagine her sitting by her candle in the Karroo desert, following the humble old Zulu parson, Kumalo, from his Griqualand valley to Johannesburg as he goes in search of Ab-

James Stern, "Out of Africa," *The New Republic*, vol. 118, no. 12, March 22, 1948, pp. 28–29.

salom, his only son. Tens of thousands of African natives have left their families and hills for Johannesburg, for under Johannesburg there is gold—the gold which has broken up every tribal tradition, offered the native nothing in place of those traditions, and driven men of all colors to drink, madness and murder.

When Kumalo discovers that gold has made his brother into a "politician" who fears to speak the whole truth, his sister into a prostitute and his son into a thief, he can only turn to his God. But when he learns that Absalom, out of fear, has shot dead the black people's most staunch white supporter and only son of James Jarvis, the landowner in whose valley Kumalo has his church, the old man cannot even pray. "There is no prayer left in me," he says. "I am dumb here inside. I have no words at all."

Kumalo never has many words, but he has such largeness of heart, such dignity and pity with the few at his command, that he can make men comprehend what was incomprehensible. His son imprisoned, he decides to make himself known to James Jarvis. When first confronted by the white man, he again has no words to tell the terrible news. Not knowing who Kumalo is, Jarvis prompts him:

> —You must tell it, umfundisi [parson]. Is it heavy?—It is very heavy, umnumzana [sir]. It is the heaviest thing of all my years. He lifted his face, and there was in it suffering that Jarvis had not yet seen before. Tell me, he said, it will lighten you.—Then, said the old man, this thing that is the heaviest of all my years is the heaviest thing of all your years also. Jarvis looked at him, at first bewildered, but then something came to him. You can only mean one thing, he said. . . . But I still do not understand—It was my son that killed your son, said the old man. So they were silent. Jarvis left him and walked out into the trees of the garden. . . . When he turned to come back, he saw that the old man had risen, his hat in one hand, his stick in the other, his head bowed,

Scene from the 1995 film version of Cry, the Beloved Country, *starring James Earl Jones and Richard Harris.* Videovision/Miramax/Distant Horizons/The Kobal Collection/The Picture Desk, Inc.

his eyes on the ground. He went back to him.—I have heard you, he said. I understand what I did not understand. There is no anger in me.

Jarvis holds so little anger that after Absalom is condemned to death, the white man has milk sent to Kumalo's poverty-stricken parish; he has a dam built so that the wretched soil can produce maize "standing higher than a man," and fertilizers and machines to cultivate the land. And there is so much compassion in the black man that when he looks upon the orphan girl whom Absalom has made pregnant, and sees that "nothing will come out of her at all, save the children of men who will use her, leave her, forget her. . . . Kumalo, for all his suffering" adopts her as his own daughter and takes her back home with him, so that the child of his son may not be born in Johannesburg's Shanty Town, "a great village of sack and plank and iron," where men die from diseases contracted in the heat under the earth, and women and children from coughing in the cold and rain above it.

I should like to predict that in the Reverend Stephen Kumalo, Paton has created an immortal figure. If there is a man who can read the tragedy of Kumalo's life with eyes dry, I have no desire to meet him.

The Message of *Cry, the Beloved Country* Is Hopeful

Fred H. Marcus

Fred H. Marcus was a professor of English at Los Angeles State College, now known as California State University, Los Angeles.

In the following viewpoint, Fred H. Marcus contends that the message of Cry, the Beloved Country *presents a hopeful message. He disputes critics who call Alan Paton overly sentimental, arguing that the author confronts the complexity of opposing principles in South Africa. Despite the overwhelming fear that haunts both whites and blacks, Paton is optimistic that love and compassion can overcome fear and prejudice.*

Yesterday's headlines [in late 1962] featured Little Rock, Ghana, and Johannesburg. Today, reports stream in from Oxford, Mississippi. Tomorrow, it may be an African state, a community in Louisiana, or a suburb of Chicago. Racial tensions throb in the pulse of our society. Sociologists, psychologists, religious leaders, political figures, educational spokesmen: all voice recurrent fears and hopes. The subject of race permeates our social fabric. A contemporary novelist could not escape it—if he would.

As English teachers we cannot choose but hear—and assess—novels probing into turbulent sociological and psychological depths. Yet a warning must also be sounded. If the teacher of literature is to serve his unique function of evaluating literary content, he must avoid a clear and present danger, the danger of literature becoming an adjunct, a handmaid to sociology. It is all too tempting to discuss Absalom's crime in *Cry, the Beloved Country*, go on to a more general discussion

Fred H. Marcus, "*Cry, the Beloved Country* and *Strange Fruit*: Exploring Man's Inhumanity to Man," *The English Journal*, vol. 51, no. 9, December 1962, pp. 609–16.

of Negro-white relationships, and finally leave the particulars of the novel behind while indulging in sociological speculation about opportunities for Negroes in our society and the problems faced by minorities.

Nor can English teachers clamber into ivory towers while dismissing all social content in novels. In describing his novel in 1949, Alan Paton said, "Their young men (the natives of South Africa) went astray; their old men were troubled and puzzled. Crime increased; the racial character deteriorated in the wretched hovels where the black men huddled in the slums of the white man's cities. This is the central theme of my novel, *Cry, the Beloved County.*"

Racial Problems in South Africa

The novel, then, emerges out of the racial problems in South Africa. We must assess it—not for its sociological content, nor outside its sociological content—as a work of art attempting to re-create experience in a word ordered by the writer. Lewis Gannett credits the novel with being "... unashamedly innocent and subtly sophisticated. It is a story; it is a prophecy; it is a psalm." His observations merit comment. The words *prophecy* and *psalm* imply a Biblical quality. Even a relatively unsophisticated reader will sense the Biblical roll of the language, the Old Testament–sounding place names, and the technique of sonorous repetition, in which the plaintive cry of humanity merges with a paean of hope for a brighter tomorrow. The opening sentence of Book I—a sentence repeated in the opening of Book II—combines simplicity and directness with a rhythmic pulse. "There is a lovely road that runs from Ixopo into the hills." The breaks after *road* and *Ixopo* are natural and inevitable—establishing a simple chant through intonation. If this is the beginning of a love song, a drumming yet tender cadence of geographical loveliness, the tenderness applies even to the unpleasant. The grass which is not kept, or guarded, or cared for—in the valleys where the natives live—

". . . no longer keeps men, guards men, cares for men. The titi-hoya does not cry here any more." For Alan Paton the love song remains tender, but more and more forlorn. "The great red hills stand desolate, and the earth has turned away like flesh. . . . the dead streams come to life, full of the red blood of the earth." This is a poetry of compassion, filled with wailing notes of desolation and sadness. The short first chapter closes, "They are valleys of old men and old women, of mothers and children. The men are away, the young men and the girls are away. The soil cannot keep them any more." The psalm embedded in the novel yearns forth, "Cry for the broken tribe. . . . Cry, the beloved country. . . . The sun pours down on the earth, on the lovely land that man cannot enjoy. He knows only the fear of his heart." . . .

While the details of Alan Paton's novel encourage the flaring up of anger at man's inhumanity to man, the prevalent tone is hopeful. Africans are exploited, mistreated, harried unmercifully; the whites are responsible for unfair land distribution, slum growth, unjust laws, and the disintegration of native tribal structure. Against this background of provocation, Msimangu, a black priest, speaks the most significant words of the novel: "I have one great fear in my heart, that one day when they turn to loving they will find we are turned to hating." In the baleful light of reality these words are incredible. Yet, like Steinbeck before him—whose novel, *The Grapes of Wrath*, spurred the writing of *Cry, the Beloved Country*— Paton portrays people as a wonderful mixture of toughness and tenderness, men and women who love and lose their land but are revitalized by man's unquenchable humanity.

Paradox of Love and Fear

Nor can Alan Paton be dismissed as a sentimentalist. If the attitudes above sound "unashamedly innocent," that is because Christian doctrine about loving one's neighbor is rarely consistent with practice. *Cry, the Beloved Country* confronts the paradox of love and fear co-existing in South Africa. It confronts the inevitable complexity of human beings torn by conflicting principles. For example, Msimangu, who fears the turning of love to hate, preaches with a voice of gold.

> Yet he is despised by some. . . . They say he preaches of a world not made by hands, while in the streets about him men struggle and suffer and die. They ask what folly it is that can so seize upon a man, what folly it is that so seizes upon so many of their people, making the hungry patient, the suffering content, the dying at peace? And how fools listen to him, silent, enrapt, sighing when he is done, feeding their empty bellies on his empty words.

And from Paton's point of view this picture of Msimangu has some validity. Contrasting with Msimangu in the novel is John Kumalo, a carpenter, owner of his own shop, a resident of the sinful city of Johannesburg. John stands for a more militant philosophy. He believes that ". . . what God has not done for South Africa, man must do." John understands the political and economic power structure; he recognizes the profit motive underlying the exploitation of native labor; he even recognizes the techniques of subjugation designed to keep the black man in his place. He says,

> I do not say we are free here . . . at least I am free of the chief . . . an old and ignorant man, who is nothing but a white man's dog .... the Church too is like the chief. . . . It is true that the Church speaks with a fine voice, and that the Bishops speak against the laws. But this they have been doing for fifty years, and things get worse, not better.

Complex Characters

It would be impossible not to recognize the validity of much of John Kumalo's argument. Yet, Paton presents John Kumalo as "cunning," as a self-seeking, self-aggrandizing man who seeks power but lacks courage. His "great voice growls" in his "bull throat" and he symbolizes a potential native leader with the raw power to awaken his fellow Africans. But the policemen who have heard his speeches stand relaxed. They know he can paint ". . . pictures of Africa awakening from sleep, of Africa resurgent, of Africa dark and savage. . . . But the man is afraid, and the deep thundering growl dies down. . . ." Even Msimangu concedes that many of John Kumalo's statements are true. But he perceives the essential corruption of the man's bid for power. "Perhaps we should thank God he is corrupt," he adds; ". . . if he were not corrupt, he could plunge this country into bloodshed. He is corrupted by his possessions, and he fears their loss, and the loss of the power he already has." Paton's characterization recognizes the complexity of people Msimangu—whom he approves—symbolizes a theology comfortable to Paton; John Kumalo—whom he disapproves—symbolizes a political and economic awareness attractive to Paton. Kumalo might plunge South Africa into revolt if he had the courage. Paton finds this possibility abhorrent; he hopes for evolutionary progress. Msimangu preaches golden words; yet, as a spokesman for love and religion, he represents little immediate pragmatic hope. At the end of the novel he retires to a monastic order, thus forfeiting a share in the continuing struggle. Yet even this detail contains a paradox. He will join a white communal group—thus symbolically helping to unravel another strand of the color line between men.

Early in the novel Msimangu says, "I am not a man for segregation, but it is a pity that we are not apart." The statement calls for segregation despite the speaker's demurrer. Msimangu is torn between a theoretical position disavowing segregated living and the emotional impact of real injustices with immediate impact. In one specific scene white men come to the aid of Africans. During a native boycott of buses a white man offers Msimangu and Stephen Kumalo free transportation. Later, when another white man renders the same help to black men, a policeman attempts to interfere. The white man challenges him, "Take me to court." In each of these incidents

Sidney Poitier and Canada Lee star in the 1951 film version of Cry, the Beloved Country. AP Images.

Msimangu marvels at the existence of brotherly love in action—almost as though his ritual preaching were words without application in actual instances. His incredulity belies his idealism. Stephen Kumalo's response to this latter incident conforms to Paton's affection for the innocent. "Kumalo's face wore the smile, the strange smile not known in other countries, of a black man who sees one of his people helped in public by a white man, for such a thing is not lightly done." The force of conformity to maintain an unjust *status quo* recurs in the novel. The upsetting of such conformity also recurs—thus giving support to Paton's optimism, an optimism sometimes hard-pressed by blatant injustice.

Symbolism in the Novel

One dramatic symbol in the novel helps to crystallize the South African quandary and laissez-faire solution. The language reads like a parable:

There is a man sleeping in the grass, said (Stephen) Kumalo. And over him is gathering the greatest storm of all his days. . . . People hurry home past him, to places safe from danger. And whether they do not see him there in the grass, or whether they fear to halt even a moment, but they do not wake him, they let him be.

Kumalo's statement foreshadows tomorrow's violence. The alternative to the unpleasant reality requires a love that casts out fear, a fear that flourishes among whites and blacks. The whites fear the overwhelming numbers of blacks in South Africa; the blacks fear the power of the entrenched minority. With great compassion, a compassion tinged with disillusion, Paton writes, "Who can enjoy the lovely land, who can enjoy the seventy years, and the sun that pours down on the earth, when there is fear in the heart? Who can walk quietly in the shadow of the jacarandas, when their beauty is grown to danger?" Sometimes, bitterness mutes Paton's optimism. For example, bitterness erupts in his description of foolish rationalizing.

We shall live from day to day, and put more locks on the doors, and get a fine fierce dog when the fine fierce bitch next door has pups . . . and the beauty of the trees by night, and the rapture's of lovers under the stars, these things we shall forego. We shall forego the coming home drunken through the midnight streets, and the evening walk over the star-lit veld. We shall be careful, and knock this off our lives, and knock that off our lives and hedge ourselves about with safety and precaution. And our lives will shrink, but they shall be the lives of superior beings. . . .

Paton's sarcasm draws perilously close to despair. He knows the rampant fear permeating South Africa and the foolishness it promotes; *Cry, the Beloved Country* confronts reality in detail after detail. Yet the transcending merit of the novel is its poetic rendering of experience. Paton welds incongruous elements effectively. He describes man's inhumanity to man in powerful, realistic descriptions tempered only by a vein of unsubdued tenderness. His realism is rooted in sociological and psychological insights communicated explicitly and through characterization. Secondly, he perceives love as a redeeming force; however, his faith is sometimes blunted by the realities of multiple injustices. Paton clings to a hope that good may come from evil. Out of the death of Arthur Jarvis, an indomitable force for social justice, murdered—ironically—by an African, good emerges. James Jarvis, hitherto uninterested in the problems of deterioration at Ndotsheni, catches a hint of his son's convictions. Thus, James plays a God-like role in the restoration of the small village, a role symbolizing man's capacity for change. More important, perhaps, his grandson, a "small boy with the brightness inside him," begins to learn the Zulu language and symbolizes a hope for better future relationships between black and white in South Africa.

The novel closes on an ambiguous note. Paton returns to geographical place names but invests them with obvious symbolic meaning.

> Yes, it is the dawn that has come. The titihoya wakes from sleep, and goes about its work of forlorn crying. The sun tips with light the mountains of Ingeli and East Griqualand. The great valley of the Umzimkulu is still in darkness but the light will come there. Ndotsheni is still in darkness, but the light will come there also. For it is the dawn that has come, as it has come for a thousand centuries, never failing. But when that dawn will come, of our emancipation, from the fear of bondage and the bondage of fear, why that is a secret.

Paton's symbols affirm a dawn of hope. Only the "when" is clouded. Since African natives live in the valleys, not in the highlands, the rising sun must first dispel the mists of fear hanging over those valleys. But Paton's guiding symbol, the inevitable, never-failing oncoming of light, marks his faith in evolutionary progress—geographical and human.

Cry, the Beloved Country Is Both a Call to Social Action and an Artistic Success

Edward Callan

Edward Callan studied and taught in South Africa between 1937 and 1949, first meeting Alan Paton in 1948. He was later a professor of English at Western Michigan University and wrote essays on literature for many journals and edited The Long View, *a collection of Paton's political writings.*

In this selection, Edward Callan finds that Alan Paton has created in Cry, the Beloved Country *a work that not only realistically captures the social conditions of its time and place, but also transcends them to achieve universal significance and worldwide acclaim. According to Callan, Paton's ability to tell a compelling story and his masterful use of poetic language combine to make Paton's first published novel a unique classic. The theme of* Cry, the Beloved Country, *Callan explains, is social disintegration and the need to restore a moral order. Paton's solution is not social, but individual—he recognizes the need for personal responsibility in addressing social ills.*

Africa has seen extraordinary political change since *Cry, the Beloved Country* was written in 1946. . . .

In the 1980s a new generation has grown up in Africa, and this generation faces challenges and tensions that differ greatly from those of the immediately postwar colonial period (including the problem of the continued presence of *apartheid* on the continent). Therefore no novel written in the 1940s is likely to reflect with any exactness conditions now prevailing in Africa; and Paton's *Cry, the Beloved Country* is no exception. But it is still true to say that this novel portrays with remarkable authenticity a segment of South African life during a brief period following the end of World War II. The work succeeds—and it still appeals to a very wide readership—because Paton effectively endowed his regional portrait with a measure of universal human significance. The realities of the postwar South African setting in which the events of the novel take place were in all likelihood unfamiliar to most readers; but the theme of social disintegration, and the countertheme of the need to restore, could evoke sympathetic understanding in a world exhausted by war. These themes are worked out in the novel through two complementary actions: Stephen Kumalo's physical search for his son, Absalom, and James Jarvis's intellectual search for the spirit of his son, Arthur. In each case, the journey, once undertaken, leads to an inner, spiritual awakening.

Universal Significance

The story that sustains these deeper themes and contrasts is a very simple one. Stephen Kumalo, aging Zulu pastor of a small Anglican mission church in the tribal village of Ndotsheni, sets out for the unfamiliar world of industrial Johannesburg to seek his sister Gertrude, who had gone there, years before, to look for her husband and had not been heard from again. He hopes also to discover his son, Absalom, who went to look for Gertrude and failed to return. And he has the further hope of finding his brother, John, who, like so many others from the village, had gone to Johannesburg and had not returned. He finds all three. But each is enmeshed in a web of moral degeneration, and his hopes of reuniting them in the old close-knit tribal family are defeated.

He finds his son, Absalom, a confessed murderer. The victim is Arthur Jarvis, a young white man noted in Johannesburg for his devotion to the cause of racial justice, and the only son of James Jarvis, the white farmer whose land occupies the fertile high ground above the barren, eroded valley of Ndotsheni. Between the discovery of the murder and the completion of the trial, the paths of the bereft fathers cross. Each seeks to understand his son's divergence from accustomed ways—the one fallen from the standards of the church his father served, the other committed to a vision of racial justice quite alien to his father's conventional assumptions. The elders return home, the wiser, if sadder, like T.S. Eliot's Magus, "no longer at ease in the old dispensation." Their mutual recognition of each other's suffering engenders a hitherto unthought-of sense of shared humanity. So simple a narrative framework can achieve literary significance only to the degree that a writer finds a fitting artistic vehicle for the depth of his vision and the power of his initial emotional mood.

Moral Purpose

Novelists, while engaged in composition, struggle to reconcile a desire to represent some human situation truthfully, with a desire to arrange their materials in the best, and most interesting, order. For some writers, the technical matters of style and arrangement are a primary concern. Others, impelled by the urgency of their concern with the human situation, adopt fictional or dramatic forms to express heartfelt convictions. While it is also a successful artistic achievement, *Cry, the Beloved Country* is a product of this second urge, which Paton once described as a desire to write "books that would stab South Africa in the conscience." He draws attention to the moral aspect of his purpose in his "Author's Note" on fictional persons and events, when he states: "In these respects therefore the story is not true, but considered as a social record it is the plain and simple truth."

In the light of the broad facts of the South African social record in 1945–46, the period of the novel's setting, this claim is certainly justified. Even those who did not share Paton's views on race relations would admit that the conditions encountered by the aged Zulu priest, while searching for his son, really existed. It was true that the land in tribal reserves, like the countryside around his tribal village, Ndotsheni, was poor, badly eroded, and incapable of sustaining its people; that the tribal reserves were inhabited chiefly by old men and women because the young men were away working in the mines and the industries of Johannesburg; and that overcrowded urban slums and lack of opportunity for employment contributed to growing frustration and crime.

There seems little doubt, therefore, that Paton turned to literary creation in a Trondheim [Norway] hotel, in part out of nostalgia for his homeland and, in part, impelled by the urgency of what he had to say about social and moral disintegration in South African black society. An article of his that appeared in *Forum*, 15 December 1945, almost on the eve of his departure for the tour of Europe and the United States during which he wrote *Cry, the Beloved Country*, is of particular interest in this regard, for it shows that the basic theme of the novel was uppermost in his mind. This brief article, "Who Is Really to Blame for the Crime Wave in South Africa?" is remarkable for two reasons: first, for the urgency of its tone; and second, because it contains the essential themes of *Cry, the Beloved Country*, prior to their embodiment in fictional form.

Paton began his article on crime by warning against the tendency to dismiss outbreaks of crime among Africans as part of a general postwar phenomenon, thereby ignoring the more important underlying cause, the disintegration of tribal society under the impact of Western economy and culture. . . .

The second part of the article turns to the question, "How is society to be restored?" And it responds: "Moral and spiritual decay can be stopped only by moral and spiritual means." . . .

Besides focusing on the general climate of disintegration, *Cry, the Beloved Country* draws on other realities of the South African social condition of 1945–46. . . .

In *Cry, the Beloved Country* these include the building of Shanty Town, the bus boycott, the discovery of rich new gold deposits at Odendaalsrust, and the air of frenzied excitement that the discovery engendered on the stock market and in Johannesburg as a whole. The actual record also included such less publicized endeavors as the work of the Anglican clergy, both black and white, at the Mission House, Sophiatown; and of the welfare workers at Diepkloof Reformatory and at "the wonderful place," Enzenzeleni, where the blind were rehabilitated. . . .

Fear Is Central Theme

Cry, the Beloved Country also probes the no less real problem of the subconscious springs of racial attitudes that, tinged with "the bondage of fear," inhibit justice and the inclination to restore. It reveals one fear in particular, diagnosed by the thoughtful young Zulu priest, Msimangu, who had no hate for any man. Speaking of the whites he says: "I have one great fear in my heart, that one day when they turn to loving, they will find we are turned to hating." The intensity and pervasiveness of this fear is one of the central themes of the novel. Fear shows in the eyes of the God-fearing as well as of evildoers. There is fear, too, in the daily newspapers. The land itself is enveloped in fear. And fingers of fear reach toward the future: "Cry, the beloved country, for the unborn child that is the inheritor of our fear. Let him not love the earth too deeply." Commenting on this passage more than thirty years later in *Towards the Mountain*, Paton said that if the child loves the earth too deeply he cannot ask immunity from pain: "This is what the visitors from America and Britain and Germany and other countries mean when they say to me, 'Ah, but your country is beautiful.' They mean, 'But why is it so full of pain?'" And he adds: "I am sometimes astonished when I remember that these words were written in 1946, and that it took many of the white people of South Africa thirty years to acknowledge their truth, when black school children started rioting in the great black city of Soweto on June 16, 1976, on the day after which, of all the hundred thousand days of our written history, nothing would be the same again." In his first novel, where these events of 1976 were unforeseen, the intense concern with a climate of fear nevertheless heightens the dramatic conflict of love and hate; for many of the characters know, or come to know, that fear engenders hatred, and that only through love can fear be cast out. . . .

Voices of South Africa

It is not surprising that Paton wrote *Cry, the Beloved Country* quickly, since he already had all the material in mind. What is surprising, however, is that he wrote it so well. The stroke of genius was his hitting upon a lyric and dramatic framework— none of it thought out in advance—that could incorporate more than the realistic "slice of life" ordinarily offered by novels of social purpose like those of [John] Steinbeck or [Knut] Hamsun. From the perspective of Trondheim the whole of South Africa lay before the artist's inner eye like a map. He could envision the landscape of Natal beloved from childhood, and the contrasting bustle of Johannesburg, the City of Gold, a magnet for Africans from tribal areas seeking a new way of life. Even more significant than the landscape spread out before his mind's eye was the din of remembered voices on his inner ear—South African voices talking incessantly about problems—problems of race, problems of language, and problems of separate living space. *Cry, the Beloved Country* is, in fact, a book for the ear rather than the eye. There are many works of art that incorporate a multitude of voices, from Greek tragedy, with its choruses comprising "the voices of the people," through Chaucer's many-voiced Prologue to the *Can-*

terbury Tales to the multitude of voices in James Joyce's *Ulysses* and his medley of tongues in *Finnegans Wake*. What all these have in common is their mingled lyric and dramatic method; for a multitude of voices cannot be incorporated in discursive prose. Paton, then, did not superimpose a poetic, or lyrical, prose style on the social theme of his novel; rather he composed the novel of lyric and dramatic elements because, artistically, there was no other way to embody his powerfully felt emotion.

The essential interest in *Cry, the Beloved Country* lies in the compelling story that unfolds through the action of the plot; but three other artistic qualities combine to help make it an original and unique work of art: first, the poetic elements in the language of some of the characters; second, the lyric passages spoken from outside the action, like the well-known opening chapter; and third, the dramatic choral chapters that break the sequence of the story for social commentary, but nevertheless widen the horizons of the action to embrace the whole land. There are three such chapters, in particular: Chapter 9, a chorus of African voices; Chapter 12, a chorus of white voices; and Chapter 23, which is a mingled chorus on justice. . . .

Kumalo's Quest

The plot of *Cry, the Beloved Country* combines three related quests corresponding largely to Book One, Book Two, and Book Three of the work itself. Book One, the Book of Kumalo, is concerned at first with the physical quest of the Reverend Stephen Kumalo, who travels from the African village of Ndotsheni to Johannesburg in search of his sister Gertrude, his son Absalom, and his brother John, who have all "disappeared" in the metropolis. His guide to these regions of lost people is another Anglican priest, a fellow Zulu of wholly different background, the Reverend Theophilus Msimangu. Msimangu, as has been pointed out, is a man with a deep philosophic bent and clear logical mind whose secular hero was the sharp-witted philosopher Alfred Hoernlé. He guides Kumalo down among the lost people as Virgil guided Dante through the infernal regions, opening his eyes and his understanding to the meaning of enigmatic things. . . .

Book Two is the Book of James Jarvis, father of the murdered man. He sets out from the closed mental world of his own habitual assumptions and prejudices and seeks to understand the liberal spirit revealed to him in his son's reputation and writings. Again, on the analogy of Virgil [leading] Dante, James Jarvis, "seeking his way out of the fog into which he has been born," is guided by the voice of his dead son who had "journeyed . . . into strange waters" and set down his philosophy in "A Private Essay on the Evolution of a South African."

Book Three is the Book of Restoration. In it, the physical and psychological quests of the earlier books turn toward the spiritual path of redemption. This is the region where, after guiding him through the horrors of hell and the mount of purgatory, Virgil left Dante to proceed alone with no guide but love. . . .

Actions Bring Restoration

The theme of restoration pervades Book Three on several levels. There is a beginning made on the restoration of the land through the work of a young agricultural demonstrator; there is the restoration of Kumalo's leaky village church through the generosity of James Jarvis; and this, in turn, is a halting step towards the restoration of brotherhood—one human being reaching out toward another across the barriers of fear and prejudice. The climax of the theme of spiritual restoration is reached when Kumalo, who in Book One neared despair, makes his lone pilgrimage to the mountaintop to share his son's agony on the morning set for his execution. . . .

Paton's *Cry, the Beloved Country* offers no blueprint for a utopian society. It offers instead recognition of personal responsibility. The crucial development in the characters of both Jarvis and Kumalo is that each comes to recognize how individual fear or indifference infects society with moral paralysis; and that the antidote for this paralysis is individual courage willing to go forward in faith. They do not wait, therefore, for some miraculous healing of this paralysis to be brought about by the direct intervention of God, or through the implementation of some scheme for a final solution, or through the flowering of the promises of some manifesto. They act by taking whatever steps are possible to them as individuals in the immediate present. A road taken in faith has no certainty of arrival; if it did, faith would be unnecessary. *Cry, the Beloved Country* therefore, rightly concludes with an acceptance of uncertainty: "But when the dawn will come of our emancipation, from the fear of bondage and the bondage of fear, why, that is a secret."

The Political Vision of *Cry, the Beloved Country* Is Naïve

Stephen Watson

Stephen Watson is a South African poet, educator, and literacy critic. He is currently a professor of English at the University of Cape Town and director of the Writing Center. Among his works are Cape Town Days *and* Critical Perspectives on J.M. Coetzee.

In the following viewpoint, Stephen Watson accuses Alan Paton of sentimentality in Cry, the Beloved Country *and finds the book politically naïve. For Watson, the fundamental difficulty is that Paton attempts to solve the material problem of detribalization with a metaphysical solution involving love and compassion. Watson contends that the roots of South Africa's problems are political rather than ethical and the solutions Paton offers are far off the mark.*

Paton wrote his first and most famous novel at a time when liberalism still seemed to provide an answer to South Africa's problems. In a sense, it represents the culmination of the heyday of white liberal optimism and confidence during the two or three decades preceding the novel's publication, and it is deeply informed by the thinking of South African liberal intellectuals like [Alfred] Hoernlé, [John David] Rheinalt-Jones and J.H. [Jan Hendrick] Hofmeyer.

This "Story of Comfort in Desolation" was written when the English United Party was still in power in 1948; and it presents a picture of optimism, together with an assumed confidence in the European's ability to lead and guide Africans to a better condition. Today it is regarded by many who would have praised it then as an old-fashioned paternalist

Stephen Watson, "*Cry, the Beloved Country* and the Failure of Liberal Vision," *English in Africa*, vol. 9, no. 1, May 1982, pp. 29–44. Reproduced by permission.

book, which portrays Africans in a sentimental and unrealistic light; and it is probable that Mr. Paton himself, who has since become much more deeply involved in politics (in common with other liberal writers) would agree. Soon after *Cry* was written the Afrikaner Nationalist Party came into power, and liberals have been forced into a more militant and committed position.

This was written in 1957 by an anonymous reviewer in *The [London] Times Literary Supplement*. Yet even when the novel was written, roughly ten years earlier, the liberal vision which finds frequent didactic expression in it was inadequate. The very problems which *Cry, the Beloved Country* first formulates and then endeavours to solve do not admit of a solution in the terms, which liberal ideology provides.

A Literary Mode of Tragedy

If Paton's intentions in *Cry, the Beloved Country* are carefully examined, it will emerge that his primary concern in this novel is to expose a certain state of affairs in South Africa; namely, the social consequences of the destruction of the tribal system by the whites and the general disintegration, both moral and otherwise, which characterizes South African society as a whole. Through the personal sagas of the Reverend Stephen Kumalo, James Jarvis, and their respective sons, he wishes to reveal some of the tragic consequences of this social disintegration and, at the same time, to provide an example of moral and spiritual growth through suffering—a Christian message of comfort and hope despite the prevailing desolation—and to make an appeal to the liberal consciences of his readers.

In order to achieve these purposes, Paton makes use of the literary mode of tragedy. But this is not only because the novel abounds in those fateful contradictions which make tragedy the most appropriate mode for it. As J.M. Coetzee has said:

A favoured mode among White South African writers has been tragedy (though Afrikaans writers have given much time to a mythographic revision of history). Tragedy is typically the tragedy of inter-racial love: a White man and a Black woman, or vice versa, fall foul of the laws against miscegenation, or simply of White prejudice, and are destroyed or driven into exile. The overt content of the fable here is that love conquers evil through tragic suffering when such suffering is borne witness to in art; its covert content is the apolitical doctrine that defeat can turn itself, by the twist of tragedy, into victory. The tragic hero is a scapegoat who takes our punishment. By his suffering we undergo a ritual of expiation, and as we watch in sympathy our emotions are purged, as Aristotle noted, through the operations of pity and terror.

Tragedy affords a solution, both artistic and otherwise, to that which in reality has not been solved at all. Coetzee goes on to say:

> Religious tragedy reconciles us to the inscrutable dispensation by giving a meaning to suffering and defeat. . . . The predominant example of religious tragedy in South Africa is Alan Paton's *Cry, the Beloved Country.* A young African comes to the city, falls among bad companions, and in a moment of confusion kills a White. He is hanged. The fathers of the dead men console and learn to respect each other. The hero who bears the blows of fate is here doubled in the persons of the two fathers; we share their suffering as they share each other's suffering, in pity and terror. The gods are secularized as the pitiless justice of the law. Nevertheless, Paton's fable bears the invariant content of religious tragedy: that the dispensation under which man suffers is unshakeable, but that our pity for the hero-victim and our terror at his fate can be purged by the ritual of re-enactment.

It is not, however, only because of its apolitical nature that tragedy becomes a mode which results in mystification rather than revelation. In the final essay of *Language and Silence,*

Mangosuthu Buthelezi of the Inkatha Freedom Party shakes hands with ANC president Nelson Mandela as South African president F.W. de Klerk looks on in Pretoria on April 19, 1994. This was an attempt to put an end to political violence in the country. AP Images.

George Steiner, discussing whether revolutionary art will succeed in producing 'high' revolutionary tragedy, remarks:

> no less than a tragedy *with* God, with a compensating mechanism of final justice and retribution, a tragedy *without* God, a tragedy of pure immanence, is a self-contradiction. Genuine tragedy is inseparable from the mystery of injustice, from the conviction that man is a precarious guest in a world where forces of unreason have dark governance. Lacking this belief, a drama of conflict will hardly be distinguishable from serious comedy, with its pattern of intrigue and mundane resolution (the equations of tragedy cannot be solved, there are in them too many unknowns).

Tragedy Depends on Mystery

Sophoclean tragedy, for instance, draws much of its mystery and strength, its power to evoke feelings of pity and terror, from its characteristic emphasis on the gap between human and divine judgements. Sophocles writes throughout in the conviction that the laws of the gods are not the same as the laws of men, and what may seem right enough to men may be utterly wrong for the gods. His tragic world is one in which men, acting according to their human nature, are countered and corrected, for evil or for good, by powers outside themselves, and although they may try to work against these, in the end they are at their mercy. The ways of the gods remain a secret and it is not for men to criticize them or even to hope to understand them. What is required is a mood of unquestioning awe and respect. The discrepancy between a divine order and the order of the world is what creates genuine tragedy.

Now it would seem that Paton, in order to make a powerful emotional appeal to the consciences and liberal sentiments of his readers, is concerned to make the causes for the tragic unfolding of events which his novel records ultimately inexplicable, the function of some Fate or divinity whose ways cannot be fathomed by man. For only through this strategy will injustice become mysterious and produce that sense of ultimate mystery which is one of the defining features of tragedy. Consequently, he is continually harping on mystery and the mysteriousness of human existence. The novel abounds in expressions of this sort:

> Who indeed knows the secret of the earthly pilgrimage? Who indeed knows why there can be comfort in a world of desolation?

> His son had gone astray in the great city, where so many had gone astray before him, and where many others would go astray after him, until there was found some great secret that as yet no man had discovered.

> I believe, he said, but I have learned that is a secret. Pain and suffering, they are a secret. Kindness and love, they are secret.

> Why was it given to one man to have his pain transmuted into gladness? Why was it given to one man to have such an

awareness of God? . . . But his mind would contain it no longer. It was not for man's knowing. He put it from his mind, for it was a secret.

And just as many aspects of human existence are surrounded by a nimbus of mystery, so the law is deified, is put into a position where it cannot be questioned; it is treated as a divine institution which requires unquestioning awe and respect as an utterly objective arbiter over the subjective follies and anarchies of men:

> You may not smoke in this Court, you may not whisper or speak or laugh. You must dress decently, and if you are a man, you may not wear your hat unless such is your religion. This is in honour of the Judge and in honour of the King whose officer he is; and in honour of the Law behind the Judge, and in honour of the People behind the Law. When the Judge enters you will stand, and you will not sit till he is seated. When the Judge leaves you will stand, and you will not move till he has left you. This is in honour of the Judge, and of the things behind the Judge.

Paton's Tragedy Fails

Yet in attempting to re-create the mystery of injustice and Fate which has such potent emotional effects, Paton stumbles into the contradiction which Steiner has pointed out. For the series of misfortunes which his novel relates are definitely not the result of the obscure workings of gods (or of God) whose ways and whims cannot be discovered by man. Like the law which has been formulated as an expression and defence of the interests of white South Africa alone, and which therefore has no credibility whatsoever as an impersonal god, these misfortunes are quite explicable in terms of the man-made reality and historical conditions of South Africa in the first half of this century. *Cry, the Beloved Country* is thus a tragedy of "pure immanence" on top of which a mystifying Christian concern with suffering and joy has been imposed. In short, it is not genuine tragedy at all.

Part of Paton's technique of mystification is to portray a succession of unfortunate events and then to dwell on the deep, passive grief which these cause in various persons. Thus, in the section which dramatizes a housing shortage in the townships outside Johannesburg and which refers to the death of a black woman's child and to her subsequent grief, we find generalizations of the following sort: "Such is the lot of women, to carry, to bear, to watch, and to lose." Thus we repeatedly find Stephen Kumalo with his "tragic eyes" and "his face in the mould of its suffering." The description of the misfortune is invariably converted into a drawn out characterization of the almost insuperable sorrow and mourning which it arouses. And although Paton could be said to follow this strategy in order to convey the very real helplessness and justifiable bewilderment of the simple-hearted, largely uneducated black in the face of a cruel and alien white world whose domination is ubiquitous and so unfathomable that, like a Kafkaesque one, it takes on all the mysteriousness and arbitrariness of an unknown god, the function of his emphasis on blind, grief-stricken reactions is both to obscure the real reasons (and hence possible solutions) for the tragic incidents and to elicit from the reader a purely emotional identification with the suffering hero so that, again, the real reasons for a predicament are smothered under the flow of sympathy which the reader feels. [Playwright Bertolt] Brecht's "estrangement" effects, whereby the emotional responses of his dramatic characters are deliberately muted in order that the audience might better perceive that a particular bereavement has specific societal causes and thus can be prevented through specifically social solutions (which perception might make possible a rejection of the fatalities and eternal recurrences of tragedy), might have had a salutary effect on *Cry, the Beloved Country.* For the emotionalism of the novel time and again results in mystification.

An Unresolved Tension

There is another type of mystification at work in this novel, one which has equally serious consequences. As a rule, a novel opens by depicting a problematic situation which the rest of the text then seeks to solve. Another way of putting this would be to say that the text (whether it be novel, poem, or drama) is internally dissonant. In the words of [author] Terry Eagleton, it is "never at one with itself, for if it were it would have absolutely nothing to say. It is, rather, a process of *becoming* at one with itself—an attempt to overcome the problem of itself." In its simplest, most conventional expression, this dissonance usually takes the form of a conflict between the dreams and idealism of an individual, and a society whose materialism and determinism prevent the fulfilment of individual ideals. The internal dissonance of the text is produced by a conflict between material-historical conditions and the various forms of necessity which these impose, and an ideology which enshrines values opposed to those determined by these conditions.

Cry, the Beloved Country, provides a particularly clear example of this process which is characteristic of almost all literature. The problem that it initially poses and presents is that of the detribalization of blacks by whites and the lawlessness and moral corruption which this enforced social disintegration has caused. The novel describes quite accurately and also explains a certain historical phenomenon which is now a commonplace in the analysis which one finds in South African criminology textbooks. Msimangu formulates the central problem of the novel as follows:

> The tragedy is not that things are broken. The tragedy is that they are not mended again. The white man has broken the tribe. And it is my belief—and again I ask your pardon—that it cannot be mended again. But the house that is broken, and the man that falls apart when the house is bro-

ken, these are the tragic things. That is why children break the law, and old white people are robbed and beaten.

And this is set out more formally in the papers of the murdered Arthur Jarvis:

> The old tribal system was, for all its violence and savagery, for all its superstition and witchcraft, a moral system. Our natives today produce criminals and prostitutes and drunkards, not because it is their nature to do so, but because their simple system of order and tradition and convention has been destroyed. It was destroyed by the impact of our own civilization. Our civilization has therefore an inescapable duty to set up another system of order and tradition and convention.

It is this social disintegration which constitutes the central problem to which the novel addresses itself.

At the same time, however, a certain ideology, which is an amalgam of liberalism and Christianity, is brought to bear upon this problem. And it is through this that the internal dissonance of the novel becomes most apparent; it is through this, too, that the major mystification of *Cry, the Beloved Country* is perpetrated. Through the mouthpieces of Stephen Kumalo and Msimangu, Paton attempts to solve what is clearly and statedly a material, sociological problem by means of metaphysics; against the multiple problems caused by detribalization and urbanization he advances the solution of love. Thus Msimangu maintains that "there is only one thing that has power completely, and that is love. Because when a man loves, he seeks no power, and therefore he has power." Of course this is useless; the problem has not been caused by a lack of love in South Africa, and therefore to prescribe an antidote of love for it is simply naïve and beside the point. The actual problem and Paton's solution for it are two completely separate, independent spheres which have no real practical relation to each other. And since there is no possibility of the one really acting upon the other, since crime cannot be solved through love, and also because Paton can see no other solution (his ideology prevents this), throughout *Cry, the Beloved Country* there is a steady displacement of or shift away from the major problem of the book, the sociological one, and an increasing focus on a single consequence of it: the personal sufferings of Stephen Kumalo and, to a lesser extent, James Jarvis. The focus steadily shifts away from the question of what has caused a certain state of affairs and what is to be done about it, and increasingly revolves around the efforts of single individuals to survive and to transcend personal suffering. And since the problem cannot be solved by the Christian love of Msimangu or Kumalo, nor by the liberal change of heart which James Jarvis undergoes and which expresses itself through a paternalistic handout to a "boy's club" and his financial assistance in the restoration of the valley, it is simply subsumed under the religious trials of Kumalo and the symphonic finale to the novel. . . .

Naïve Political Vision

Now it is all too clear that throughout *Cry, the Beloved Country* Paton is preaching for a revolution of hearts ("Change from Within") rather than for a revolution in social and economic structure ("Change from Without"). Because of his liberal Christian vision and the limits it automatically imposes on the nature and range of political beliefs and practices available to him, he never really questions the power of humility, respect for persons, compassion and the quest for personal salvation to achieve a significant restructuring of society. He himself does not seem to realize (though John Kumalo makes this clear) that although Christianity might offer profound spiritual strength to people at bay (the novel itself is a good illustration of just this), it also imparts a political weakness which dictates, however necessarily and realistically, an acceptance of the hegemony of the oppressor. Nor does Paton ever really question the applicability of the Sermon on the Mount to a political programme. For though it may be possible to establish just relations between individuals purely by moral and rational suasion and accommodation, in inter-group relations this is practically an impossibility. The relations between groups are always predominantly political rather than ethical; they are determined by the proportion of power each group possesses as much as by any rational and moral appraisal of the comparative needs and claims of each group. Paton, with an ideology which commits him to the individual rather than to the group, does not understand this.

Nevertheless, scattered through the novel are a number of passages which either implicitly or explicitly call into question his ultimate faith in a change of heart (an increase in love and the rooting out of fear and hatred) to cure various ills. . . .

In so far as *Cry, the Beloved Country* records an antagonism between a basically materialist view of South Africa's conflicts (which is reflected in John Kumalo's attitudes and ideas) and an idealist attempt to solve them (reflected in the ideas of Stephen and Msimangu), it can be regarded as a rudimentary novel of ideas. But Paton never develops this antagonism to the point where it would become truly meaningful. Indeed, he cannot; his ideology prevents him from doing so. Through his liberalism and Christianity which demand that people be judged as ends in themselves and not as means, and according to their moral worth and integrity rather than their practical usefulness, he can conveniently dispose of this antagonism. Thus John Kumalo's *moral* corruption is emphasized to the extent that his actual political worth, the substantial accuracy of his many brief analyses, are ultimately ignored and glossed over: "—Perhaps we should thank God he is corrupt, said Msimangu solemnly. For if he were not corrupt, he could plunge this country into bloodshed. He is corrupted by his possessions, and he fears their loss, and the loss of the power he already has." In short, because John Kumalo is not a good man, his politics are not good. Yet, ironically, he is the one person in the novel who displays something of a real political understanding.

The immediate result of this ideological clash being dissolved and disposed of through moral condemnation is that the final political vision which emerges from *Cry, the Beloved Country* is naïve in the extreme.... [The practical "solutions" offered by Paton] scarcely solve or even begin to suggest a way of solving the problematic historical situation with which the novel deals.

Overly Sentimental

A still further result of this failure to develop the implications of this clash of ideologies is an artistic failure; the novel becomes badly weighted, lop-sided; it becomes a tear-jerker—which is only another way of saying that it is lacking in reality. Its sentimentality is, of course, in accord with one of its express intentions; significantly, *Cry, the Beloved Country* is subtitled "A Story of Comfort in Desolation". Like a good liberal and Christian, Paton is always concerned to console, to lessen any potential conflict, and to appeal to the moral consciences and emotions of his readers. Depictions of pain are always the best means for this latter purpose since they provoke pity and sentimentality. And his liberal desire to reduce conflict perhaps explains his almost obsessive presentations of the *good* white man, of characters like the advocate who takes on Absalom Kumalo's case *pro deo*, Father Vincent, and those helping blacks at a school for the blind: "It was white men who did this work of mercy, and some of them spoke English and some spoke Afrikaans. Yes, those who spoke English and those who spoke Afrikaans came together to open the eyes of black men that were blind." Furthermore, he uses this figure of the *good* white—the liberal hero (Arthur Jarvis), who is destroyed by the harsh South African reality—as a representative figure who atones through his death for the collective guilt of the whites. For the purposes of conciliation he also uses the figure of the *good* black man, the "Uncle Tom" character, who will allay the suspicions and the hostility of whites towards blacks. But the paternalism implicit (and often quite explicit) in his treatment of blacks and all the emotional effects aroused by his attempted reconciliations do not have the final effect of providing comfort in desolation; they merely serve as an incomplete disguise for the limitations in the ideology which informs the novel. In the final analysis, *Cry, the Beloved Country* does not so much display the iniquities of various aspects of South African life; rather, it reveals the poverty of Paton's ideology.

Cry, the Beloved Country Is Racist

Patrick Colm Hogan

Patrick Colm Hogan is a professor of English and comparative literature at the University of Connecticut. He is the author of several books, including The Politics of Interpretation: Colonialism and Cultural Identity.

Patrick Colm Hogan's discussion of Cry, the Beloved Country *in the following selection focuses on how he uses the novel to help students think critically about stereotyping in a work of fiction. He cites* Cry, the Beloved Country *as an example of racist thinking that is not inspired by race hatred. Hogan contends that* Cry, the Beloved Country *is a blatantly paternalistic novel, and he is incredulous that the* New Republic *could have deemed it "one of the best novels of our times." He claims that Alan Paton presents whites as possessing knowledge, while blacks are able to succeed only by deferring to whites.*

Many works of postcolonial literature engage in a critique of dominant national ideologies and the hierarchies those ideologies sanction. When teaching such works, I usually begin by distinguishing and explaining some varieties of ideological critique. In doing this, my aim is twofold: (1) To help students understand the author's criticisms of dominant views, and (2) to help students think critically about positive claims set forth by the author as alternatives to those dominant views. First of all, I distinguish "external" and "internal" forms of critique. By "external," I mean forms that seek to reject the entire social structure in which a given ideology is

Patrick Colm Hogan, "Paternalism, Ideology, and Ideological Critique: Teaching *Cry, the Beloved Country*," *College Literature*, vol. 19/20, no. 3/1, October 1992–February 1993, pp. 206–10. Copyright © 1992–1993 by West Chester University. Reproduced by permission.

located. . . . By "internal critique," I mean forms that seek to criticize one part of the dominant ideology by using another part of that same ideology or which criticize actual social practices on the basis of their incoherence with common ideological claims. These can be straightforward representations of hypocrisy that take no stand on the ideological principles in question, as in much of [Ghanaian writer Ayi Kwei] Armah's *The Beautyful Ones Are Not Yet Born*, or they can be more politically ambiguous treatments that both undermine and support, criticize and celebrate the system they are representing. Works of this last variety "deconstruct" one dominant position but build up their own views on the same basis, rigorously maintaining the problematic, staying within the limits of "reasonable" discourse in which the dominant ideology is located.

Cry, the Beloved Country Is Racist

Alan Paton's *Cry, the Beloved Country* is an excellent example of this final, ambiguous type of critique. As it is a novel of South Africa, the ideological concerns to which Paton addresses himself are centrally concerns about race: the condition of blacks, the relations between the white minority and the black majority, etc. But it is within a largely racist problematic that Paton defines his critique of South African racism. Thus, I preface class discussion of this work with a brief introduction to racist ideology. Students, even graduate students, know of race hatred and prejudice, hiring discrimination, and the like. But most of them—and I include here black American students, nonwhite students from postcolonial countries, and others who suffer the effects of racism—have not considered the ways in which racist thinking is typically structured. Indeed, many of them are only dimly aware that racist beliefs need not involve race hatred, just as many are only dimly aware that sexist beliefs need not involve misogyny.

First of all, racist (and sexist) ideology is always based on an affirmation of difference. Though much recent theory obscures this fact, the first function of ideology justifying oppression is to establish a firm distinction between the oppressor and the oppressed. Nazis did not rationalize the Holocaust by claiming that Aryans and Jews were the same, nor did American slaveholders defend slavery by asserting that blacks and whites share a universal humanity. Fascists, slaveholders, colonialists, patriarchs all seek to justify their domination by reference to deep and abiding differences that radically separate people on the basis of skin color, sex, national or class origin, etc., and that effectively dehumanize members of the oppressed group.

However, not all dehumanization is the same. While there are many variations on this theme, there are three particularly common motifs. Drawing on the work of [leading Indian-born social and cultural writer] Ashis Nandy and others, I point out that members of an oppressed group are most frequently portrayed as subhuman/animal, prehuman/juvenile, or posthuman/aged. Each of these types carries with it a cluster of properties defining members of the oppressed group in terms of their sexuality and instinctual life, intellectual capacities, morality, social formations, verbal abilities, stature, color, and miscellaneous physical attributes. In addition, each is typically associated with a range of images and metaphors which are appropriate to the putative bestiality, juvenility, or senility of the oppressed group. As it is the juvenile category which is most relevant to *Cry, the Beloved Country*, I will skip the others and outline it briefly. . . .

Blacks as Juvenile

The juvenile stereotype is first of all the assimilation of members of the oppressed group to children, with the correlate assimilation of the oppressing group to adults. It separates these groups by stage of development, knowledge, maturity—but not, as with the bestial stereotype, by species. There are two common subtypes of the juvenile stereotype: the adolescent and the puerile. The puerile is asexual or presexual, rowdy perhaps but neither instinct-driven nor moral, playful rather than violent or rational, innocuously anarchic, chattering, small, cute. Members of a puerile group need basic education and the firm, loving guidance of the dominant, "parental" group. This is a common patriarchal characterization of women, and a standard characterization of colonial natives during times of peaceable relations. The adolescent, in contrast, is sexually irresponsible, overpowered by instinct, morally confused, violent, prone to delinquency, rough and deceptive in speech. This shares with the bestial stereotype a characterization of the oppressed group as sexual, violently criminal, and anarchic, but the degree is less in each case and the origin of these tendencies is in upbringing, not biological nature; thus the appropriate response to delinquency is a social equivalent of reform school and severe, rather than affectionate, parenting.

Both of these stereotypes were common in the ideology of "the white man's burden," and they remain common today in liberal views of black South Africans and black Americans. It is important to emphasize that a consistent practice based on such stereotypes can be part of a critique—a specifically liberal critique—of a dominant ideology which views members of the oppressed group as subhuman, rather than merely prehuman. Arguing that whites can and should educate and elevate blacks opposes the idea that blacks are innately inferior, that the appropriate treatment of blacks is punishment rather than (ideologically sound) education, etc. Advocating gallantry towards "ladies" involves, when sincere, active opposition to rape, harassment, and physical abuse. However, at the same time, child stereotypes remain solidly within the problematic which defines and justifies oppression; they reaffirm the superiority of white people and white culture or men and male culture, the absolute necessity of white or male domination—at least until that indefinite point in the future when the childlike blacks and women have matured. Thus they provide an interesting case of ideological critique aimed at the dominant ideology, but nonetheless open to further ideological critique aimed at the underlying problematic. They define, simultaneously, a paternalistic ideology and a paternalistic critique of ideology.

Most of this theoretical material I deliver in lecture to the students, though I do elicit examples and even some stereotype properties from them. Having presented these ideas, however, I encourage the students to analyze the work on their own, with less direct guidance from me. As I cannot adequately reproduce the development of class discussion, I will simply indicate some of the topics I bring up for discussion and some of the points which arise in that context.

Paternalism in *Cry, the Beloved Country*

The first thing I ask students is very simple: who are the good characters in the novel? After discussion, we find that they are of two sorts: (1) Blacks who have devoted their lives to Christ, and (2) whites who help blacks, prominently including the director of a reformatory for black adolescents. We can see immediately how the latter group functions to critique one form of racist ideology, by holding up benevolent whites as figures to be emulated. This is consistent with Paton's genuine criticism of the common treatment of blacks as animals—of which students can usually give many textual examples. But something else is already implied by the fact that the good black characters are virtually all devout Christians: the cultural superiority of Europe over Africa.

What are some examples of this in the novel? It is easy enough for students to find cases. Father Msimangu explains that he cannot "hate a white man" because "It was a white man who brought my father out of darkness." Another character, told that he has "a love for truth" explains that "It was the white man who taught me." Indeed, the association of Africans with darkness and Europeans with light is ubiquitous in the book. A particularly striking case is at the white-run school for the blind. Speaking of this school, Father Msimangu tells Father Kumalo, "It will lift your spirits to see what the white people are doing for our blind." And later, Father Kumalo thinks, "those who spoke English and those who spoke Afrikaans came together to open the eyes of black men that were blind"—his words having both literal and metaphoric resonance. Even the native languages receive their only genuine value from Christianity, as when Father Kumalo finds "the Zulu tongue . . . lifted and transfigured" through a translation of the Bible.

Thus whites have light, vision, truth, knowledge, and they can guide blacks—help them, educate them. But what of black leaders? Who are the black leaders in the book? First of all, there are the priests. In addition, there are examples of tribal leadership and secular political leadership. Father Kumalo's brother John is the primary instance of a black secular leader. He is corrupt and deceitful, and betrays his brother and nephew at the first opportunity. Moreover, if he were not corrupt, Father Msimangu explains, he would be worse; he would not solve problems, but "plunge this country into bloodshed." The tribal chief, on the other hand, is an ignorant fool, who tries to take over the direction of land development from whites, but quickly shows that he has no knowledge, no understanding, no capacities. Thus black leaders fall into four categories: (1) those who are corrupt, (2) those who provoke senseless violence, (3) those who are incompetent, (4) those who are devout Christians. Moreover, even members of this last group are able to lead only by deferring to whites: by accepting European religion, by rejoicing in the help offered by whites to blacks ("Kumalo's face wore the smile, the strange smile not known in other countries, of a black man when he sees one of his people helped in public by a white man"), by standing aside as the whites work out land development plans (unlike the tribal chief), by encouraging ordinary blacks to collaborate with the police, etc. Indeed, the narrator and the black characters are quite explicit in granting only whites adequate intelligence for leadership. For example, Kumalo is good and sympathetic, but painfully simple. And Father Msimangu speaks of four leaders, one European, one of mixed European and African descent, and two African: "Professor Hoernle . . . he was the great fighter for us . . . he had Tomlinson's brains, and your brother's voice, and Dubula's heart, all in one man." Africans may have deep feelings, or deep voices, but only the Europeans and those with European blood have "brains." (Though ultimately of the same general category as Kumalo—a black man filled with Christian love, who can act for the good if led by whites—Dubula is a secular activist and thus a partial exception to the preceding schema. . . .)

Black Delinquency as White Responsibility

And what of ordinary blacks in this book—what are they like? They are murderers, thieves, bootleggers, and prostitutes. And the novel repeatedly tells us that these crimes—not the casual brutalization of black men and women, not the denial of political and economic rights to the overwhelming majority of the population—are the big problems in South Africa; they are, after all, the problems of Kumalo's own family, and, more importantly, they are crimes which affect whites. The narrator informs us about one region where "most of the assaults reported were by natives against Europeans." As Father Msimangu laments, today "children break the law, and old white people are robbed and beaten," and as Father Kumalo reflects, on the edge of despair, "His son had gone astray. . . . But that he should kill a man, a white man!" And what is the cause of these problems? Again, it is not political oppression and economic exploitation. Rather it is the lack of an adequate familial structure in which a strong moral tradition can be handed down—and specifically the failure of Europeans to provide such a system, their failure to accept parental responsibilities.

The clearest statement of this paternalism is in the fragment of a treatise left behind by Arthur Jarvis, the absent hero of the novel, the great fighter for blacks who was killed by black criminals, a man directly associated with two other murdered liberators, Abraham Lincoln and Jesus Christ. Here, I ask my students to analyze the excerpt of Jarvis' writing in detail, for in this passage the novel's paternalism is fully explicit. Jarvis insists that the destruction of native culture was "permissible" because of that culture's "violence and savagery . . . its superstition and witchcraft." But because of this destruction, "Our natives today produce criminals and prostitutes and drunkards." He continues, "Our civilization has therefore an inescapable duty to set up another system of order and tradition and convention." In this context, students typically discuss the implicit characterization of the native peoples as "our" children—puerile or adolescent—whom "we" (i.e. whites) have the right and duty to educate and reform. In addition, we discuss other presuppositions of the fragment, for example that contained in Jarvis' reference to South African resources as "our great resources," where the "our" clearly refers to Europeans.

Depending on the class, we might conclude by discussing the reception of the novel. Why would *The New Republic* refer to this as "one of the best novels of our time," and why would it be such a bestseller, a novel still required reading in some American high schools? Ideally, I would eventually lead this into a discussion of the function of liberalism and paternalism, not only in South Africa, but in the United States as well, where the debate over minorities tends to be defined within quite comparable parameters. Even when we find the ideological complicity of Paton's paternalistic critique—its strict adherence to a racist problematic—quite obvious, many of us may still fail to recognize a similar complicity in writings on race by prominent white American liberals. While it is valuable to help students understand the operation and critique of dominant ideology in any context, it is most valuable when they can apply and extend that understanding within the context of their own society.

Paton Has a Complex View of Good and Evil

Carol Iannone

Carol Iannone teaches in New York University's Gallatin School of Individualized Study and has published in numerous journals, including Commentary *and the* Antioch Review.

In the following viewpoint, Carol Iannone acknowledges that after its initial success, reviewers criticized Cry, the Beloved Country *for its sentimentality and propaganda. She disputes these critics, saying that Paton rejects easy answers and has a complex understanding of how good and evil interact in history. Iannone specifically states that Alan Paton is not "so shallow" as to propose boys' clubs as a solution. Paton admired democracy in the United States, and Iannone draws parallels between the racial struggles in South Africa and the early civil rights struggles in the United States.*

At the time of [*Cry, the Beloved Country*'s] publication, Alan Paton (pronounced with a long a) was a forty-five-year-old principal of a black reformatory school. He was born in 1903 in Pietermaritzburg, Natal, a colony of Great Britain until the South African union was formed in 1910, joining Natal and the other British colony, the Cape of Good Hope, with the two Afrikaner republics, the Transvaal and the Orange Free State. His parents were associated with the fundamentalist Christadelphian sect, but in general Paton matured in the kind of Victorian-Edwardian-Anglican ambiance that seemed to define a lot of English South Africa at that time, a world of now old-fashioned virtues like "manliness, decency, honor," as Paton's biographer, Peter F. Alexander, names them.

Carol Iannone, "Alan Paton's Tragic Liberalism," *American Scholar*, vol. 66, no. 3, Summer 1997, pp. 442–51. Copyright © 1997 by Carol Iannone. Reproduced by permission.

Christianity's Centrality

Having skipped a few grades, Paton entered Natal University College at age sixteen and graduated with a Bachelor of Science degree. There he met Railton Dent, an older student and the son of a missionary; Dent became the greatest individual influence on Paton's life by imparting to him "one thing," as Paton explains it, "that life must be used in the service of a cause greater than oneself." Paton goes on to elaborate: "This can be done by a Christian for two reasons: one is obedience to his Lord, the other is purely pragmatic, namely that one is going to miss the meaning of life if one doesn't." It proved for Paton to be the prescription for a long and industrious life, full of service, courage, and accomplishment.

If reading the life of the average twentieth-century literary figure can make us glad we are not like its subject, reading about Paton's can make us wish we were. Christianity was central to Paton's life from first to last. He left the Christadelphians to become a Methodist, and then in 1930 he became an Anglican, joining the church of his wife, Dorrie, whom he married in 1928 and with whom he had two sons. He was eventually to become a lay leader and to participate in the church's repudiation of racialism and separatism.

After graduation from college, Paton taught white children for some years and became increasingly active in Christian benevolent organizations. In 1934 he fell deathly ill with enteric fever, lost over a third of his body weight, and was confined to a hospital and convalescent home for six months. When he recovered, a friend told him that after such an experience he would not be able to resume his old work, and this proved to be true. Under the direction of Jan Hofmeyr, one of South Africa's liberal Afrikaner statesmen, the Department of Education was undertaking the transformation of both black and white reformatories from virtual prisons to something closer to schools.

Paton was put in charge of Diepkloof, near Johannesburg in the Transvaal, where he was responsible, at different times, for from 360 to more than 600 black pupils, officially aged nine to twenty-one and called "boys" at both the white and black institutions. They had been committed for offenses ranging from pilfering fruit from street stalls to rape and murder. Here he worked veritable miracles of humanization, with the help of an enlightened supervisor at the ministry, several sympathetic outside government overseers, and an excellent staff whom he largely trained himself.

Writing Career Takes Off

Paton had always shown a literary bent and had been writing poetry and attempting novels since his college days, but the pressures of work and family prevented him from bringing any mature work to fruition. After twelve years at Diepkloof, this was to change. In 1946, he embarked on an extended journey to review correctional institutions in Europe, the United States, and Canada. One September at twilight, he found himself sitting in Norway's Trondheim cathedral, admiring its beautiful rose window and longing for home. He went back to his hotel and began writing, completing in three months as he continued his trip the novel that was to become *Cry, the Beloved Country*. He gave the manuscript to the friends whom he was visiting in the United States; they were much and tearfully taken with it, suggested changes, and found a publisher, Scribner's, where Maxwell Perkins, the editor for Ernest Hemingway, F. Scott Fitzgerald, and Thomas Wolfe, advised acceptance. In appreciation for their efforts Paton granted his friends a generous percentage of what were to be the novel's considerable profits thereafter, and Scribner's went on to be the American publisher of the rest of Paton's twenty or so books, including two more novels, *Too Late the Phalarope* and *Ah, But Your Land Is Beautiful*, a book of short stories, a play, two volumes of autobiography, two biographies, some devotional literature, and several collections of essays, poems, stories, and political writings, much of it interesting and even important, but none quite the equal of his exquisite first novel.

In later years, Paton often observed that South Africa had very little to unite it—what with myriad African tribes, a population of Indians and "coloreds," and two different white "races," all with separate languages, cultures, histories, values, and symbols. South Africa's union had been brought about by war and politics more than by shared ideals. Only the physical land itself might inspire common loyalty. As Maxwell Perkins observed, the land is one of the chief characters in *Cry, the Beloved Country*. The novel opens with a lyrical description of the spectacular landscape of the Ixopo district in Natal. . . .

Interplay of Good and Evil

The novel's success may have been due, in part, to the moment of South African history that it captured, 1946, before the imposition of "grand apartheid" was to consume the country completely in politics. The depression and war had passed. Industrialization and urbanization were breaking down tribal customs, even as the increasing population of blacks and whites in the cities was worsening the tensions under separatism. The novel strips away the surface assurances of white supremacy to reveal what has in some respects become a wasteland—a literal wasteland in the case of the sordid slums and the dying tribal lands, but also a spiritual wasteland, characterized by alienation and mistrust among races and peoples and families and generations. "It is fear that rules this land," says Msimangu, one of the black priests who helps Kumalo.

So painful is the reality depicted in *Cry, the Beloved Country* that when the playwright Maxwell Anderson adapted the novel for the stage (with music by Kurt Weill), he called it *Lost in the Stars*, and made it a cry against a God who had abandoned his creatures. This was done much to Paton's consternation. His perspective is thoroughly Christian, though in the sense of a struggle for the light, not in the application of received truths. The novel manifests both Christian and tragic qualities. The final answers are "secrets" and "mysteries" that reside only with God, and at any given moment the divine may not be evident or clear. The characters must bear up in the face of desolation, injustice, pain, and loss, but there is also hope, comfort, and consolation.

Thus despite the good liberal intentions behind the novel to move white South Africans over conditions in their society, *Cry, the Beloved Country* does not evidence the kind of superficiality that Lionel Trilling felt was typical of what he called "the liberal imagination." Avoiding easy answers, Paton enters into the perspective of both "victims" and "oppressors," and demonstrates a humility and acceptance before the unknown and unresolvable. . . .

Paton's rejection of easy racial moralism does not mean that he exonerates the South African system. Far from it. But he doesn't go in for the blanket indictment of South Africa that became typical in later years. Msimangu castigates the white man for giving "too little . . . almost nothing" to the blacks, but he also acknowledges the gift of Christianity and appreciates the good white people who do what they can. On the other side, the fiery speech of John Kumalo demanding higher wages makes a lot of sense, notwithstanding the menacing anger that informs it.

Arthur Jarvis's Understanding

In one of Arthur's writings, a work in progress discovered by his father after his death, Paton provides a lengthy version of his own thought, though skillfully tailored to reflect Arthur's younger, more naive understanding. Arthur carefully distinguishes what was "permissible" from what was "not permissible" in South Africa's history. Reflecting an earlier understanding of colonialism, he does not feel it necessary to delegitimize all of white South Africa:

What we did when we came to South Africa was permissible. It was permissible to develop the great resources with the aid of what labour we could find. It was permissible to use unskilled men for unskilled work. But it is not permissible to keep men unskilled for the sake of unskilled work.

It was permissible when we discovered gold to bring labour to the mines. It was permissible to build compounds and to keep women and children away from the towns. It was permissible as an experiment, in the light of what we knew. But in the light of what we know now, with certain exceptions, it is no longer permissible. It is not permissible for us to go on destroying family life when we know that we are destroying it.

This aspect of the novel has perhaps not been fully appreciated. Paton had a tragic grasp of the way good and evil are interwoven in human history. In Arthur Jarvis he created a character who understood the inevitability of civilizational progress and expansion and the conflict and loss that they bring. At the same time, Arthur insists that the colonizers take responsibility for the damage they have done in the process:

> The old tribal system was, for all its violence and savagery, for all its superstition and witchcraft, a moral system. Our natives today produce criminals and prostitutes and drunkards, not because it is their nature to do so, but because their simple system of order and tradition and convention has been destroyed. It was destroyed by the impact of our own civilization. Our civilization has therefore an inescapable duty to set up another system of order and tradition and convention. . . .

Transcends Didacticism

After initial widespread adulation, critics began to find fault with *Cry, the Beloved Country*, seeing it as sentimental and propagandistic, more a treatise than a work of art. The novel tends to survive these objections, however, because the whole is greater than the sum of the parts. Wherever one probes a weak spot, the novel resists at some other point; as Lewis Gannett put it, it is "both unabashedly innocent and subtly sophisticated." The mythic narrative involving the search for the lost son blends with a realistic picture of a modern society. The novel's earnest idealism is offset by the amorphous sense of fear that pervades the country and by the suppressed fury the characters carry within them. Kumalo and Msimangu can erupt in anger and yield to subtle cruelty, and the brows of the young official at Diepkloof are constantly knitted against the difficulty of his work. (Paton's own increasingly tight-lipped expression was his response to the frustrations he faced.)

Where *Cry, the Beloved Country* grows too fable-like, it suddenly turns analytical; where too discursive, it waxes poetical. Edward Callan, Paton's chief critic, has done a thorough job of delineating Paton's techniques, but, at the same time, it is not necessary to overstate the novel's purely literary pretensions in order to appreciate its achievement. Dan Jacobson, the self-exiled South African novelist, put *Cry, the Beloved Country* above strictly literary, political, or moral considerations into a category of works he called "proverbial."

Behind much of the criticism of Paton's novel one can make out a political edge. Early objectors to the novel tended to be white South Africans who bridled at its grim portrayal of black life. When the first film version was shown, the wife of the nationalist Afrikaner politician D.E. Malan remarked, "Surely, Mr. Paton, you don't really think things are like that?" The novel was not permitted in the schools until a few years before Paton's death [in 1988]. Later objections came from black militants and their sympathizers, who saw the novel as an expression of white liberalism and mocked Paton's belief in boys' clubs, for example. But the author was not so shallow as to imagine that boys' clubs per se were the ultimate solution to South Africa's dilemma. Paton makes clear in the novel that the renewed ameliorative efforts in the aftermath of the tragedy are a good beginning: but "when that dawn will come, of our emancipation, from the fear of bondage and the bondage of fear, why, that is a secret."

Actions Supported Convictions

Nevertheless, Paton was modest enough to appreciate the good such measures could do. Paton personally paid for the education of countless black youngsters, gave financial help to many others who were in need, and contributed enormous amounts of time and money to his church, to charitable organizations, and to institutes working for social improvement. These commitments expressed his larger conviction that, as he said elsewhere, "the only power which can resist the power of fear is the power of love"—that the only way to achieve justice in South Africa was through a change in the hearts of enough people to make a difference. The militants who faulted Paton for proposing "love" as a solution to social and political injustice did not seem to realize how much of the groundwork for their political activism had been prepared through voluntary organizations of the kind Paton labored in and supported.

So, too, with the novel itself. Noting the blows it took from later militants, the black South African novelist Richard Rive defended *Cry, the Beloved Country*, calling it a "watershed" in South African fiction in that it brought the racial question into literary purview and widely influenced later writers. The Angolan writer Sousa Jamba read the novel at age fifteen in a second-hand copy that smelled of kerosene because, he surmised, its previous owners had stayed up nights to read it. Jamba carried it with him everywhere, and "forgot that what I was reading was written by a white man."

Even disdainful black writers such as the South African poet Dennis Brutus had to admit the novel's power and influence. And while deploring much in the characterizations, Ezekiel Mphahlele, another South African writer, concedes that *Cry, the Beloved Country* is "the first work in the history of South African fiction in which the black man looms so large." Although he did not like the portrait of the humble Zulu priest (preferring the angry John Kumalo instead), Mphahlele implicitly admits that it was true to life.

In Stephen Kumalo, Paton has painted a full picture of an African man, a good but flawed human being, complete with an inner life and a moral compass. The judge's sophisticated legal reasoning in no way surpasses the rural parson's own horrified grasp of his son's murderous act. Furthermore, Paton portrays his black characters in the dignity of individual responsibility even as he shows the restricted circumstances in which they must maneuver.

Paton's preoccupation with individual responsibility must partly have been derived from his experience at the Diepkloof Reformatory, where he stressed education, introduced extensive vocational training, and made many improvements in diet, clothing, sanitation, and living conditions. He became famous for successfully putting into practice the theories of experts in juvenile delinquency who believed that freedom could be used as an instrument of reform and rehabilitation. . . .

Turning to Politics

The point is that while Paton did believe that the "root causes" of black crime lay in conditions in South Africa, for which whites were largely responsible, he also knew what painstaking care, what investment of self, and what demands on the individual black person were involved in undoing the effects of these causes. He knew that even his best efforts did not always succeed; with all the good he was able to accomplish at Diepkloof, he was never able to eliminate corporal punishment entirely. All this gave him a kind of clear-eyed wisdom that served him well in his activities after 1948.

To the surprise and consternation of many, the 1948 elections saw the defeat of the relatively liberal United Party un-

Canada Lee as Kumalo in Cry, the Beloved Country. AP Images.

der the great Boer War general and statesman Jan Smuts and with him his liberal ministers, in favor of the Afrikaner Nationalist Party under D.E. Malan. The Nationalist victory, combined with the success of his novel, convinced Paton to leave Diepkloof, where the new regime would eventually undo all his work. He tried for a while the life of a man of letters.

But the worsening political situation in the country and his commitment to service, as well as his relative lack of literary inspiration following his first success, led him to politics. . . .

In 1953 Paton helped found the Liberal Party to uphold the hope of a non-racial South Africa, and he wrote and spoke extensively on behalf of its principles, both at home and abroad, even after the Party itself was proscribed in 1968. (All reports portray him as an electrifyingly gifted orator.) The Liberal Party was against violence and staunchly anti-Communist, and its classical rights–based premises differed from the socialist Freedom Charter of the African National Congress. During these years Paton lost his wife to emphysema, endured a miserable period of widowerhood, and, fortunately, married his second wife, Anne, in 1969.

Paton's politics can make us wonder how "wishy washy liberal" ever became a common epithet. His liberalism was a matter of strength and courage all the way through. He discarded his early and rather casually accepted racialism as he came to see, in the face of the majority white view, that white supremacy was at odds with Christian theology (and was driving South Africa toward disaster). Later, he maintained his moderation against the growing radicalism around him— again, at least partly because of his religious understanding.

Resisted Idealism and Radicalism

As Paton's biographer Peter E. Alexander points out, the whole metaphor of Paton's two-part autobiography, *Towards the Mountain* and *Journey Continued*, suggests that Christian perfection is not something to be had in this world, but only to be worked toward. Paton was an idealist, but not a political utopian. He was aware of the built-in limitations in South African society and was patient with incremental change. For this reason he was to fall into disfavor as the racial activism in his country became more fierce, but he stood fast against enormous pressure, mockery, and contempt. The attacks were not only on him but on liberalism itself and came from blacks and whites, including many former allies. On speaking tours in the United States, he encountered the vociferous anti-apartheid opposition on American campuses that branded him a paternalistic relic.

Paton angered the radicals in three areas, writes Alexander. One, he opposed trade sanctions in the 1980s because he felt that they would hurt the black poor most of all. To this we can add another reason: his experience at Diepkloof, which had taught him that punishment did not lead to true reform; he continued to believe in the need for moral suasion to lead people to free and enlightened choice. He also continued to hold out against violence, although he testified for mercy in the sentencing of Nelson Mandela. Two, he gradually came to favor federalism instead of a unitary state, at least as a transition to one man one vote for South Africa. And, three, he admired Chief Buthelezi, a fellow Christian but, for the militants, a thorn in the side.

Paton took plenty of heat from the government during these years. Although, as the author of *Cry, the Beloved Country*, he was spared arrest and banning, his passport was temporarily revoked, his mail opened, his phones tapped, his house searched, and his property damaged. At certain times he was watched and followed; he received ugly threats and letters from white racists. But his quarrels with the militant left are perhaps of greater interest today.

Paton demanded to know where the "young white Radicals who sneer at liberals and liberalism" would have been without previous liberal efforts. They "would have been in darkness until now," he asserted. "One cannot measure past labour in terms of present demands." He went on to caution that "if black power meets white power in headlong confrontation, and there are no black liberals around, then God help South Africa. Liberalism is more than politics. It is humanity, tolerance, and love of justice. South Africa has no future without them." Paton's fictional character, Msimangu, says something similar, though more lyrically, in one of the novel's most memorable lines: "I have one great fear in my heart, that one day when they turn to loving they will find we are turned to hating."

Admired the United States

Paton often compared the South African situation with the American. He admired the United States as an example of democracy to the world and wrote that American citizens "should go down on their knees and thank God for their Constitution, their Bill of Rights, and their Supreme Court," since, he felt, these had prevented the United States' racial problem from exploding like South Africa's and resulting in cycles of all-out oppression and violence. He was also canny enough to recognize the difference in demographics. To righteous white outsiders who demanded "moral solutions to political problems" he dryly remarked that it was easier to be good when you are secure—that is, when you are the majority.

Paton's tendency to compare the United States and South Africa invites several observations today. In some ways, the two countries are the positive and negative of each other. Aside from an almost exact reversal in racial demographics, South Africa, according to Diana Wylie, an American academic writing in the *Yale Review* of her recent visit to South Africa, is without common narratives or unifying myths or founding principles to unite its disparate peoples and is struggling to reach for them now. We have such common narratives and principles and are doing our best to delegitimize them. The idea of preserving different groups in separate enclaves was one of the delusions of Afrikaner nationalism, and tribalism and ethnicity persist as problems in the new South African state, while here we disfavor the old assimilative American model and energetically promote ethnicity and separatism under the rubric of "multiculturalism." If South Africa watched tribal breakdown and did nothing to remedy its effects, we watch family breakdown and do nothing. Finally, Wylie notes that Christianity has and continues to be a unifying force in South Africa. In contrast, our rights enthusiasts labor to strip religion from the public square.

Although Paton's political labors and political writing pretty much overshadowed his literary work after *Cry, the Beloved County*, and his two later novels show the strain of politics, he did manage to produce a few fine stories and an important biography of Hofmeyr. But it was his supreme and lasting achievement to uphold a model of humanity in the face of suffering and injustice and to have limned it in an extraordinary and enduring novel.

Paton harkens us back to the moral discipline of the early civil rights struggle in our own country, and he stands for something lost in our post–civil rights era of radicalized demands, grievances, and entitlements: the tragic sense, the mature recognition that "suffering is an inescapable part of life" and that human character is formed in response to it. He held to the belief that love is greater than hate, and that persuasion and reason are better than force and intimidation. He never lost the to us now perhaps distant conviction that "a man who fights for justice must himself be cleansed and purified." He resisted the simplified ideologies of both Left and Right. His liberalism was not the narcissism of good intentions, but the lifelong commitment of a man who saw reality whole.

Cry, the Beloved Country claims our attention through its unembarrassed simplicity, its nuanced complexity, and its textured beauty, as well as through the qualities of mind of an earlier age that it manifests, a turn-of-the-century belief in the dignity of the individual, a modest acceptance of the limits of the human condition, and an affirmation in the power of reason, faith, and goodness. As such it commends itself to the turn-of-another-century's end.

Paton Depicts the Breakdown of Tribal Order in *Cry, the Beloved Country*

Harold R. Collins

Harold R. Collins taught English at the University of Connecticut at Waterbury.

In this viewpoint, Harold R. Collins contends that the desolation in Cry, the Beloved Country *is caused by the loss of the old tribal customs that gave morality to African lives. In order to help the reader better understand detribalization, Collins cites the fiction of Joyce Cary and Elspeth Huxley because these novels also deal with the breaking of tribes. He finds that Alan Paton has dealt honestly with a complex situation and gives the reader true insights into life in apartheid-era South Africa.*

Alan Paton's *Cry, the Beloved Country* has been published in Scribner's attractive "Modern Standard Authors" series and is now [in the early 1950s] being studied in college classrooms. There are, of course, several difficulties standing in the way of an informative discussion of this fine novel. Fiction about Africa may conceivably be terra incognita for us. We remember [Joseph] Conrad's great story, *The Heart of Darkness*, but that belongs to the earlier era of the scramble for Africa. Olive Schreiner's rather overrated *Story of an African Farm*, conscientiously reread, turns out to be a feminist novel which scarcely mentions the Africans. We need more information on social conditions in the Union of South Africa than is available in Paton's capsule history of the country, quoted by Lewis Gannett in his useful introduction to the Scribner's edition. More specifically, we need reliable information on race rela-

Harold R. Collins, "*Cry, the Beloved Country* and the Broken Tribe," *College English*, vol. 14, no. 7, April 1953, pp. 379–85.

tions in South Africa and the rest of Africa, so we may confidently demonstrate the novel's power and integrity in dramatizing racial problems in terms of human feelings—human hopes, aspirations, fears, and sorrows. Nonfiction works on Africa are legion, but many of them are superficial travelogues, and those that look like serious, impartial studies may grind the imperialist ax.

Tribal System Gave Moral Guidance

Cry, the Beloved Country is a "story of comfort in desolation." We shall observe that the desolation consists not so much in the crowded native reserves, or the ruin of the reserved land by erosion and overcropping, or the absence of the young men drawn to the mines, or the frightful living conditions of the town natives—terrible as these afflictions are—but in the loss of the old African moral order that gave purpose and meaning to African lives. When Gannett says that *Cry, the Beloved Country* "creates rather than follows a tradition," he is probably putting his case rather too strongly. At any rate, the African novels of Joyce Cary and Elspeth Huxley are helpful toward an understanding of Paton's novel because they are tragedies, or tragicomedies, on the conflict of cultures in Africa and because they treat of the breaking of the tribes which results from that conflict. Likewise, in the jungle of information and special pleading on African conditions, there are dependable nonfiction sources, especially anthropological studies, that document the theme "Cry, for the broken tribe, for the law and the custom that are gone."

We recall that the Zulu preacher's sister Gertrude goes to Johannesburg to find her husband and becomes a prostitute there, that his son Absalom, sent to the great city to find the sister, falls among evil companions, becomes a thief and a murderer. Arthur Jarvis, whom Absalom murders, has been a prominent *kaffirboetie* (or friend of the natives). His bereaved father finds among his son's manuscripts what seems to be an address on native crime, ironically, an explanation of the high incidence of crime among the Africans in the towns:

> The old tribal system was, for all its violence and savagery, for all its superstition and witchcraft, a moral system. Our natives today produce criminals and prostitutes and drunkards, not because it is their nature to do so, but because their simple system of order and tradition and convention has been destroyed. It has been destroyed by the impact of our own civilization. Our civilization has therefore the inescapable duty to set up another system of order and tradition and convention.

Detribalization Takes Its Toll

Indeed, one of the most important effects of European civilization in Africa is the deterioration and breakdown of the old African cultures and the consequent breakdown in African personalities. In the past our observation of the striking differences between these native African cultures and those of the Western world, and, perhaps even more, our feelings of racial superiority, have blinded us to the fact of the moral force of the old order. Now we begin to understand what has been happening. In the twentieth century, especially outside the reservations, in the mining compounds, the squatting grounds on the white men's farms, and the native slum "locations," Africans have been "detribalized," as the technical term has it. They have been losing the old moral standards without assuming, or being able to assume, those of the white men. Like Absalom and Matthew Kumalo, they have become social derelicts almost completely without moral guidance of any sort and, naturally enough, criminals.

Before the tribes were broken, the Africans had a good deal of moral guidance in their traditional religions. As an experienced missionary and expert on the West African peoples says:

The behavior of Africans is not left to uncharted freedom, but is governed by a system of rules and regulations, so extensive, so complicated, that Europeans who study it stand amazed, and are tempted to declare the Africans to be the slaves of tribal custom. . . . The riotous instincts are restrained by forces that are not of this tangible sphere. In other words, the ethics of the Africans, their customary morality is grounded in their religion.

In the Kumalos' Zululand the old African religion has gone forever, though witchcraft has not. Absalom and the pitiful young girl he lives with are "Church of England," but their religion has no real hold on them. Their morality is not grounded in Christianity, certainly.

Anyone who wants to learn about detribalization would do well to consult *Africa*, the journal of the International Institute of African Languages and Cultures, which specializes in studies of the problems of culture contact. In this journal we find anthropological studies that confirm Paton's view of the broken tribe. For instance, Miss Ellen Hellman's "Native Life in a Johannesburg Slum Yard" is a study of the conduct of Africans in an environment rather like Claremont, Alexandra, and Orlando, where Gertrude, Absalom, and Matthew Kumalo are corrupted. Her conclusions are precisely those of Arthur Jarvis—and Alan Paton:

In the drive to town families are separated from their kinfolk and form isolated groups in town. The restraints of tribal discipline do not affect the urban native, and no substitute discipline has, as yet, emerged from out the chaotic welter of transition. The old sanctions have lost their force and the sanctions which order European life are not applicable to native life.

Rejecting Christianity

Presuming that Europeans are controlled by public opinion, law, and the precepts of Christianity, Miss Hellman points out that for these Africans there is "no body of public opinion,"

Scene of members of a tribe in the 1951 film version of Cry, the Beloved Country. *AP Images.*

that conviction and imprisonment carry no social stigma because the criminal sanction has been applied to trivial misdemeanors, and that the great majority of the slum yard natives have "tacitly rejected Christianity."

For Absalom Kumalo there was "no body of public opinion" beyond the promptings of such unimproving acquaintances as his cousin Matthew, Johannes Pafuri, and Baby Mkise. Such acquaintances would not be in much awe of penal sanctions, and who can blame them, really, when an African can be arrested for some irregularity in his passes? It would seem that Absalom has "tacitly rejected Christianity" and taken his uncle's measure of his Christian father—"a white man's dog."

In a culture contact study of a group of Africans in northwestern Rhodesia [now Zimbabwe]: Audrey I. Richards gives a series of case histories of detribalized persons. The history of Jackie Biltong is representative, and Jackie reminds us of the

Kumalo boys, though the district in which he lives is an isolated one where the introduction of taxes and the money economy is just beginning to send the men to the distant labor centers, the points from which white influences radiate. Jackie's father, sacked from a job as a cook, went to the mines and took his son with him, and the woman he lived with brought Jackie up. Jackie is "smartly dressed" but somewhat disreputable and irresponsible. "Caught for pilfering," he is living on food cooked by his friend's mother and a relative of his mother. Recently he made ten shillings digging a garden for the local prostitute, and has spent the money on "clothes and beer"; he says he will "pay back friend and look for tax later on."

Novels of Cary and Huxley

The African novels of Joyce Cary, written out of his seven years' experience as a political officer in Nigeria, and those of Elspeth Huxley, an expert on African colonial affairs and a former Kenya settler, throw considerable light on the process of detribalization. Cary's novels are crowded with strayed souls, tribeless Africans free of the old African sanctions and not controlled by European sanctions. We observe what the breaking of the tribes means in terms of the disorganization of African personalities. Of course Cary is writing about Nigeria, which does not have the large white population of South Africa or the highly developed mining industry. Racial friction and the conflict of cultures are less acute in Nigeria than in South Africa. And yet, as our examples of Cary's detribalized Africans will show, the effects of breaking the tribe are much the same in the two areas.

Cary's Africans, like Gertrude, Absalom, and Matthew Kumalo, get into trouble when they leave the tribe and enter the white man's world. Henry in *An American Visitor* (1933) is a "smooth operator" who finally opens a store in the minefields and does a splendid trade in condemned and slightly blown tinned meats, secondhand caps and trousers, aphrodisiacs, smuggled gin, and abortion drugs. Ajaki in *Mister Johnson* (1947) is a cash-drawer thief. The title character of that novel is a first-rate grafter, extorting his own personal tolls on a new road and embezzling treasury funds. Like Absalom Kumalo, he inadvertently murders a man who surprises him in amateurish housebreaking.

A Loss of Culture

It might be objected that our civilized societies produce such criminals in abundance. Well, surely some of Cary's misguided Africans are peculiar to the African scene. The Reverend Seleh Coker in *The African Witch* (1936) is an irresponsible agitator and spellbinder much bolder than John Kumalo. He preaches a weird juju variety of Christian doctrine and inspires the murder and mutilation of a saintly old missionary. The fanatical and superstitious Christian converts in *Aissa Saved* (1932) provoke a riot that threatens the safety of the native officials of the local government.

Obai, Fish, and the elders of the Birri people in *An American Visitor* are so deeply distressed by their contacts with white civilization that they can only be described as neurotic. Obai's truculence toward the whites has a strange derivation. He has learned "un-Birri" ways outside his home district, and he boldly breaks a sexual taboo of his people. Then he is terrified to think that he may be denounced. His painful insecurity is partially relieved by his aggressive behavior toward the whites. Fish hates all the whites because the missionaries have given refuge to his estranged wife. Although District Officer Bewsher has tried manfully to protect the Birri from all white influences, even missionary activity, the Birri elders observe the breaking-up of the old culture; in their passionate regret for the old order passing away, they make Bewsher their scapegoat. They blame him for the "misfortunes of the time" and the "collapse of their own authority, of all decency and good behavior."

When malcontent Africans rebel against the whites, they merely give the *coup de grâce* ["blow of mercy" meant to end the suffering of a wounded creature] to their native society. Bewsher is unable to prevent a mining company from encroaching on tribal land. The Birri, feeling that they have been betrayed to the "interests," kill their benefactor and revolt. In a punitive expedition against this small, backward Nigerian tribe, only thirty natives are killed, but the old society is broken beyond repair. The old cultural forms, already badly undermined, collapse completely under the pressure of routine military operations: "The old patriarchal government disappeared and the people became a mob. Large numbers of the young men drifted away, even during the campaign, to join the flotsam of wandering laborers and petty thieves in the neighboring provinces." After the "war" Bewsher's successor finds it expedient to bring in a mission and a mining company to integrate the mob, make something like a society of it.

The tribeless Africans of the South African towns and cities belong to just such an improvised society. They are essentially a mob, and a mob rejecting the standards of white public opinion, white law, and Christianity.

Loss of Social Order and Personality

In Elspeth Huxley's *Red Strangers* (1939) the emphasis is not so much on the antisocial behavior of the tribeless Africans in the white men's sphere, as in Cary's African novels and *Cry, the Beloved Country*, but on the Africans' bewilderment in their tribal areas as they see the white intruders turn their social order upside down. This novel is an account of the effects of the British occupation of Kenya upon one family of a Kikuyu clan. For all the differences in detail such an account suggests what happened in every African community with the advent of the whites, what happened in the Kumalos' Zululand. Kenya, like South Africa, is a "white man's country" where racial friction and culture conflict are acute, though the white agricultural enterprises of Kenya do not break the tribe as quickly as the great mines of South Africa do. . . .

One might suppose that a good European education would repair the damage to the African personality wrought by the breaking of the tribe, would be the salvation of young men like Karanja, *Karioki* [two young boys in *Red Strangers*]; and the Kumalo boys. In Huxley's *The Walled City* (1948) we learn what really happens to the educated African. The Nigerian Benjamin Morris, a graduate of an English university and an editor of a small African newspaper, is hurt because the white road foreman and the white sanitary engineer pass him on the street without so much as a nod. It shames him to be patronized by "such inferior persons, who could not explain the differences between the Stoic and Epicurean schools, or outline the quantum theory." Because the Europeans are aloof, Benjamin is acutely unhappy. He loses interest in his liberal magazines from England, relapses into some of the old African superstitions, and prints the most shameless canards against the government. As long as the whites refuse to accord respect to the educated African, the very best European education cannot integrate the African personality. With a good education Absalom Kumalo might not have been a thief and a murderer, but he would have been unhappy and anti-social.

Complex Race Relations

Certainly Paton has been scrupulously fair on the "native problem." His views on the injustice of keeping Africans unskilled to support white supremacy, of developing natural resources at the expense of the welfare of African laborers, of destroying the old African tribal system and letting the Africans deteriorate physically and morally (as dramatically presented in Arthur Jarvis' address on native crime), are set in the context of the old Zulu preacher's agonizing discoveries of the degeneration of his son. Now the African novels and nonfiction sources referred to here have shown that such degeneration is commonplace in modern Africa. Moreover, none of the characters in the novel, not even Arthur Jarvis or the kindly Mr. Msimangu, has a pat and easy solution for the afflictions of South Africa. Paton honestly renders the troubled complexity of the situation—the bewilderment of the whites and Africans caught up in the baffling problems of race conflict, the confusion, the cross-purposes, the frustration of men of good will of both races. *Cry, the Beloved Country* does what no discursive work in political science, sociology, economics, or anthropology could ever do; it makes us understand "how it feels" to be a South African today; it gives us the "form and pressure" of life in South Africa.

Paton Expresses Fear for the Future of South Africa in *Cry, the Beloved Country*

J.M. Coetzee

J.M. Coetzee is a South African–born author and former professor of English literature. He has published numerous award-winning works of fiction, autobiography, and nonfiction, including Waiting for the Barbarians, Life and Times of Michael K, *and* Disgrace. *He won the 2003 Nobel Prize in Literature.*

In the following viewpoint, J.M. Coetzee dismisses Alan Paton as a "one-book man" who was never able to duplicate the success of Cry, the Beloved Country. *Coetzee muses that the acclaim Paton achieved with his first novel may have trapped him artistically. Although Paton calls for a commitment to Christian values to solve racial problems in his novel, Coetzee finds an undercurrent of fear in the novel that is at odds with the author's optimism.*

Alan Paton is best known as the author of *Cry, the Beloved Country*, a book that has probably opened the eyes of more readers to the woes of South Africa than any other. *Cry, the Beloved Country* was not only Paton's first novel, but his first book. It appeared in 1948, when he was already in his middle years. It became a best seller and brought him financial independence and fame. But in retrospect that fame now seems a mixed blessing. An obscure public servant, Paton was turned, not wholly unwillingly, into a sage and oracle, the guide for editors and interviewers in search of wisdom on South Africa. It was a role in which he remained trapped for

J.M. Coetzee, "Too Late the Liberal," *The New Republic*, vol. 202, nos. 2/3, January 8 and 15, 1990, pp. 39–41. Copyright © 1990 by The New Republic, Inc. Reproduced by permission of *The New Republic*.

much of the rest of his life. The effects can be seen not only in the increasingly ex cathedra [infallible] tone of his pronouncements, and in his tendency to think, speak, and write in brief, easy-to-chew paragraphs, but in his failure to break new ground and to develop as a writer.

Talent Stunted by Fame

Paton was born in 1903 in the province of Natal, the only province of South Africa in which people of British descent form the majority of the white population. After a decade as a high school teacher, he took over the principalship of Diepkloof Reformatory for African juvenile delinquents, where he enjoyed a remarkable career as a reformer. He transformed what had been a prison into a school, doing away with forced labor and introducing vocational education, relaxing surveillance, abolishing corporal punishment, and delegating day-to-day administration to the boys themselves. When Paton took leave from Diepkloof in 1946, it was with the intention of studying penology abroad before returning to a career in the prison service. But in Sweden [*sic*] something unplanned happened. Under the influence of what he later called "a powerful emotion," he began to write a story based on his Diepkloof experiences. Three months later *Cry, the Beloved Country* was completed.

In the remaining 40 years of his life, Paton wrote a great deal: two more novels (*Too Late the Phalarope*, in 1953, and *Ah but Your Land Is Beautiful*, in 1981, the second an embarrassingly poor piece of work), stories, memoirs, biographies, a two-volume autobiography, and a sizable body of journalism. But he remained a one-book man. His other fiction, in particular, is vitiated by a sentimentality that *Cry, the Beloved Country* escapes only by the sheer power of its sentiment. Like Olive Schreiner's *Story of an African Farm*, it gives the impression of having been written at the dictation of an overmaster-

135

ing daimon [spirit]. In both cases the writers spent the rest of their lives fruitlessly trying to recover that first fine rapture.

Not all readers of *Cry, the Beloved Country* may remember where the strange title comes from. Here is the relevant passage: "Cry, the beloved country, for the unborn child that is the inheritor of our fear. Let him not love the earth too deeply. . . . For fear will rob him of all if he gives too much." Though the novel overtly takes up a confident liberal stance, calling for greater idealism and commitment to Christian and democratic values, the experience it deals with beneath the surface is, as Paton's best critic, Tony Morphet, has argued, more troubling. The "powerful emotion" out of which the novel emerged was fear for himself and his humanity, fear for the future of South Africa and her people. Fear was the emotion that had held Paton in its grip in those hotel rooms in Sweden [*sic*] and England and the United States where he wrote the book; and the book, with its anxious ending, cannot be said to have settled his fear.

Liberalism Bound to Innocence

Back in South Africa, Paton did not confine himself to writing. His most practical and most immediately effective act was to found, in 1953, the Liberal Party, a non-racial political party that survived, in the face of continual official harassment, for 13 years, until it was legislated out of existence. Though he was a deeply committed Christian, Paton confesses that the "deepest fellowship of [his] life" was felt not in the Church but in the Liberal Party.

Liberalism, to him, was not only a political philosophy, but a creed embracing "a generosity of spirit, a tolerance of others, an attempt to comprehend otherness, a commitment to the rule of law, a high ideal of the worth and dignity of man, a repugnance for authoritarianism, and a love of freedom." In view of the forces of intolerant sectarianism, racism, and nationalism that it faced, this was, as Morphet rightly names it, "a politics of innocence." Though it never commanded the allegiance of more than a small minority of the white electorate, it did keep alive a certain spark of non-racial idealism as the fortress of apartheid began to be erected on all sides.

After the forced dissolution of the Liberal Party, Paton became a more lonely figure on the South African scene. He shared the common and perhaps blessed inability of liberals to sympathize with, or indeed even to understand, how deep sectional passions can run. He had always feared and disliked Afrikaner nationalism, and one senses in him scant welcome for the rising tide of black nationalism. He continued to hope, with less and less conviction, that fellow citizens of British descent would emerge from their slumber and exert themselves on behalf of such old-fashioned British values as respect for the rule of law (something, by and large, they have never done).

He was little attracted by the prospect of a unitary, centrally administered state such as the African National Congress promised, to be brought into being by revolution if necessary. Though he recognized that a unitary state would be "right and inevitable" if that was what the majority of South Africans wanted, and though a unitary state had in fact been part of the platform of the Liberal Party, it seemed to him that the price to pay for it would always be too high: "grief and desolation" on a huge scale. He therefore pleaded the case for a federal constitution based on universal suffrage, with effective power devolved to regions and communities. He pinned his hopes for the future on the enigmatic Zulu leader Chief Mangosuthu Buthelezi, whom he called "one of the most powerful figures on [our] political stage, fluent, extremely knowledgeable, impossible to buy," and on the kind of accommodation with whites that Buthelezi seemed to stand for.

Outdated Liberalism

On the question of action by the West against apartheid, Paton took a cautious position. In 1979 he had an interview with Secretary of State Cyrus Vance in which he counseled Vance to exert pressure on the South African government, but to do so "with the greatest skill and wisdom," lest the South Africans, concluding that by cooperating they had everything to lose and nothing to gain, went their own way, taking the country to destruction with them. But he was utterly opposed to economic sanctions. "I hereby solemnly declare," he wrote, "that I will never, by any act or word of mine, give any support to any campaign that will put men out of jobs": no goal could be grand enough to justify turning South Africa into "a starving nation." To destroy the South African economy, he argued, would anyhow be an invitation to the U.S.S.R. to intervene. On the other hand, Paton did call in 1985 for "the greatest moral and pragmatic pressure" to be brought to bear on the South African regime in the interests of its "re-education."

On the issue of sanctions, Paton had more than one exchange with Archbishop Desmond Tutu. "I don't understand how your Christian conscience allows you to advocate disinvestment," he wrote in an open letter. "I do not understand how you can put a man out of work for a high moral principle." In the same letter he congratulated Tutu on winning the Nobel Peace Prize, and added: "I have never won a prize like that. I am afraid my skin is not the right color." The comment is petty, and does not reflect well on Paton. Perhaps it is understandable: little honored in his own country, Paton was jealous of his own standing in the outside world and unhappy that the invitations and honors stopped flowing in during his later years.

Though it may seem from his statements that Paton moved to the right as he grew older, it would be more accurate to say that he stood still while the entire South African opposition, both black and white, to which he had once been central, moved left. His politics, in which a Christian commitment to nonviolence coexisted, not entirely easily, with an implacable detestation of apartheid and a hawkish anticommunism, never really changed. In the 1950s Paton had been denounced as a liberal from the right; in the 1980s the left freely used "liberal," as well as "humanist," as terms of abuse. Through it all he remained a liberal, and proud of it. Though liberalism had held the allegiance of many good people, they had never been enough, never nearly enough. As a political force liberalism had missed the boat, he knew. But in the creed itself there was nothing dishonorable. If blacks sneered at liberals, he said, it was not because liberals had ever been hypocritical or cowardly, but because they had proved themselves powerless.

Cry, the Beloved Country Opened Literary Discussion About Race in South Africa

Tony Morphet

Tony Morphet is an associate professor in the Department of Adult Education and Extra-Mural Studies at the University of Cape Town in South Africa. He writes widely on contemporary South African cultural studies.

In the following selection, Tony, Morphet traces several paths for the liberal novel in South Africa. He credits Alan Paton with opening the literary discussion about the possibility of harmony between blacks and whites. Morphet concludes that later writers, such as Nadine Gordimer, found Paton's liberalism to be backward-looking, because it was founded on an irrational faith, and rejected it.

I can recall being startled by the phrase "a world of strangers" when I first saw it in 1958 in its position as the title of Nadine Gordimer's second novel. Provocative as it was in its referential range, there was no mistaking the fact that it was intended to distinguish our time and our place from other parts of the world where people, we were to infer, were not strangers to one another. Toby Hood, the central figure of the book, a Bloomsbury Englishman "at a loose end," remarks that "in this African country" he has "come to feel curiously at home, a stranger among people who were strangers to each other."

The state policy of alienation (apartheid) had been in place for ten years when Gordimer titled her book. During the

Tony Morphet, "Stranger Fictions: Trajectories in the Liberal Novel," *World Literature Today*, vol. 70, no. 1, Winter 1996, pp. 53–59. Copyright © 1996 by *World Literature Today*. Reproduced by permission of the publisher.

same ten years the "liberal novel" had established its roots in opposition to the legal and customary terms of separation which governed the relations between people throughout the country. Alan Paton's *Cry, the Beloved Country* had, in 1948, opened a fictional discourse which sought to explore the ways in which life-sustaining bonds could be forged between people across the racialised lines of division. In setting its purpose against division and alienation, the liberal novel self-consciously assumed the burdens not only of white fear and guilt but of the formation of a redemptive consciousness as well. This is the current which ran through Paton, Gordimer, Dan Jacobson, and other white writers and which gave to the early form of the genre its narrow regional focus and its specialised intensity. . . .

The purpose of this paper is to explore the positions which this larger narrative of modernity reveals of the canonical liberal writers, and to follow from a distance the ways in which they sought to articulate their interests and identities and differences. In its procedure the paper will pick up a sequence of critical incidents, direct and indirect exchanges between writers, and use them to focus what I see as differing trajectories in the novel. Within this pattern of positions there is, I will argue, a set of exchanges, a debate, even a kind of battle, over how the conditions of life in South Africa were (and indeed are) to be represented: it is a fight which has its moral as well as its aesthetic dimensions. . . .

The "Dirty Word"

The first incident which falls within my particular focus arises in the relations between Paton and Gordimer. Peter Alexander, Paton's biographer, gives the following general account of their relationship: "Paton and Gordimer had an uneasy relationship. Paton retained his reputation as South Africa's premier novelist, despite all Gordimer's talent and energy, so that to some extent she felt the effect of his shadow; for his part he could not but be aware that by comparison with his own, her stature as a novelist was growing steadily." But the particular incident which I think illuminates much more than merely their personal awareness of each other arose out of an interview in 1974 in which Gordimer was quoted as saying, "Liberal is a dirty word. Liberals are people who make promises they have no power to keep." She announced that she would prefer to be known as a radical. To this Paton responded angrily in public print, pointing both to individual liberals and to liberal organisations which had made sacrifices precisely to keep the promises they had made, and he questioned whether "Miss Gordimer" had made similar sacrifices for her radicalism. The exchange was sharp but by no means brutal, and it is difficult at this distance to see precisely what the issue entailed except that it was one of "position"—of moral position in particular, as the criterion of sacrifice for promises makes clear; yet Gordimer's reference to the "dirty word" suggests that there were questions of aesthetic style at stake as well.

What had made *liberal* a dirty word in 1974 was not the fact that liberals were powerless (though that was self-evidently the case) but that the term had been "marked" in a very pronounced way within the Black Consciousness text, which derived its specific articulations in part from [Frantz Fanon, a psychiatrist and writer specializing in the field of post-colonial studies,] and in part from the American Black Power movement. It drew its deep resonances, however, from the "mother's milk" ideology which had grown out of three hundred years of oppression. It was a text of identity, and of difference. In its assertion of the identity of all blacks and their difference from all whites it set a challenge to the liberal propositions of cross-racial bonds of common feeling and reciprocal duties, and it did so from a position radically opposite to that of the state.

The exchange between Paton and Gordimer is important because it discloses in its brief flash the two trajectories of the "liberal novel" as they begin to figure on the landscape of global modernisation. Paton in *Cry, the Beloved Country*, his one great book, confronts the disquiet and the fear of the stranger—in himself and in his characters—and he searches for a form of transcendent meaning, which he finally grounds in religious faith and love. At the opening of the novel the old black country priest and the white farmer are aliens living together in the same place; their sons confront each other in the modern metropolis in the classic stranger encounter—mistaken action which moves to violence and to death, ultimately for both. In the unfolding of the consequences Paton brings the fathers into a common bond as neighbours bonded in shared loss and faith.

The Backward Movement

The crucial point about this trajectory is that it moves backward. It makes neighbours out of aliens. It is a return to the premodern forms of relation, not only in the sense that it is a return to the rural out of the urban, but also in the sense that it predicates the relations between the men—and hence the races—on the foundation of irrational faith. The measure of the direction can be taken from the authoritative voice which dominates the novel. It is an invented language which attempts to fuse a supposed Zulu idiom with biblical cadences in order to present itself as the direct expression of unsophisticated rural black people and, simultaneously, as the true language of the heart and the spirit.

It was this backward movement out of the experience of alienation that Gordimer recognised and rejected, and it is the same issue which was identified in the Black Consciousness reading of *liberal*. Both saw that what the situation required was a movement forward, some means of creating a world of bonds—and kept promises—beyond and ahead of the conditions of apartheid. And both views recognised that the besetting vice of the traditional liberal consciousness was an appropriation of the stranger/other into an identity which was not theirs. . . .

Paton produced only one novel of substance and power. The authority which its success gave to him closed him within a moral, political, and religious structure from which he was unable to free himself to write another of equivalent energy.

Cry, the Beloved Country's Message of Forgiveness Remained Relevant in Mandela's South Africa

Bill Keller

Bill Keller is executive editor at the New York Times. *From 1992 to 1995 he was chief of the* Times *bureau in Johannesburg. He won a Pulitzer Prize in 1989 for his coverage of events in the Soviet Union.*

In the following viewpoint, Bill Keller writes that a new film adaptation of Cry, the Beloved Country *is perfect in tone for the postapartheid era of South Africa. He finds that the novel, which was almost fifty years old at the time of filming, tells a story that has stood the test of time. The optimism expressed by Alan Paton in the novel has finally been vindicated by Nelson Mandela's release and election as South Africa's president, he concludes.*

James Earl Jones recalls that when he was offered the lead in a new film adaptation of Alan Paton's classic, *Cry, the Beloved Country*, his first reaction was: "Wouldn't that be a museum piece?"

The novel, after all, is so old that it predates the official racist order called apartheid. It has been for decades a staple of high school and college reading lists. It has been dramatized twice before, as an acclaimed Broadway musical and a rather less-acclaimed film. What can it possibly say afresh to a world that has watched South Africa's convulsive rebirth as a democracy?

But the makers of the new production, who recently concluded 12 weeks of filming here with an eye to opening at the

Bill Keller, "In *Cry, the Beloved Country*, a New Voice from the Past," *The New York Times*, December 19, 1994, p. 11. Copyright © 1994 by The New York Times Company. Reproduced by permission.

Cannes International Film Festival next May [1995], convinced Mr. Jones that in this 46-year-old standard they had found the perfect first film of the new South Africa.

They may be right. In both its light and its darkness, in its devotion to the redemptive power of reconciliation but also in its reminder that, as Mr. Jones put it, "there's a bottom to that bucket," Mr. Paton's story has much in common with the South Africa of Nelson Mandela.

"It's all about the wisdom of forgiveness," said Darrell Roodt, the South African director best known for the musical *Sarafina!*

"We didn't have to change anything," he said. "The tone is exactly the same as it was in the 1940's. If we'd made it five years ago, it would have had more of an anti-apartheid stance. But now we can tell the story with hindsight."

Cry, the Beloved Country is the story of a rural Zulu parson, Stephen Kumalo, who journeys to Johannesburg in search of his missing son and sister. In the maelstrom of the city he discovers that his sister has fallen into prostitution and his son has been arrested for the murder of a white man.

In their mutual grief at the loss of sons they never really understood, the fathers of the murderer and the murdered man become friends across the racial divide.

The book's hopefulness is held short of sentimentality by ominous reminders that the country is choosing up racial sides and running out of patience.

"I have one great fear in my heart," says the young black priest who becomes Stephen Kumalo's guide in the city, speaking of his country's whites, "that one day when they turn to loving they will find we are turned to hating."

Contemplating the current relevance of the character he portrays, Mr. Jones said: "Stephen Kumalo is a man of abiding gentleness that must be celebrated, because that's what got us to this point without the bloodshed we have seen in Somalia and Bosnia. South Africa could have gone that way."

Richard Harris and James Earl Jones, stars from the 1995 film version of Cry, the Beloved Country, *with Nelson Mandela.* Videovision/Miramaz/Distant Horizons/The Kobal Collection/The Picture Desk, Inc.

But Mr. Jones does not see the character as naive—"he is almost poetically aware"—and the actor says he balked when Mr. Roodt described the parson, in a planning meeting, as "humble."

"I said, 'I don't buy that,'" Mr. Jones mused, nursing a cup of tea at the studio north of Johannesburg where he was performing his final scenes. "Gentle, I buy. Humble to me means you give away something of yourself. I think he's a very selfish man. He's as selfish as Christ was; he's saying gentleness can work, and he's going to impose it on everybody."

Upon its publication in 1948, the book's success was instant and beyond Mr. Paton's wildest hopes.

"In my 35 years of publishing I have never known the like," Charles Scribner, the publisher, wrote to the novelist. By the time Mr. Paton died in 1988, over 15 million copies had been sold in 20 languages, including Zulu. For many Americans, it was a first exposure to the drama at the southern end of Africa.

Mr. Paton, whose life as a writer, educator and politican is the subject of an engrossing new biography by Peter F. Alexander (*Alan Paton: A Biography*, Oxford University Press), fell out of favor with many campaigners against apartheid. He opposed tactics like trade boycotts and came to favor the idea of a federation of ethnic states as a stepping stone toward majority rule.

But even harder-edged writers like Nadine Gordimer, who had little use for white liberals, praised *Cry, the Beloved Country* for its part in waking up the outside world.

By Mr. Paton's lights, the two previous efforts to dramatize his masterwork were failures.

The 1951 British film directed by Zoltan Korda is recalled mainly as one of the earliest appearances of Sidney Poitier, playing the young Soweto preacher who showed Stephen Kumalo around the urban jungle. Mr. Paton found the movie plodding, for which he, as a partner in the screenplay, was partly to balme. The movie was a failure at the box office.

Released three years after the National Party won control and began implementing its draconian scheme of racial division, the film unavoidably became something of a political tract.

"It was a bit too much on the nose," Mr. Roodt said. "It was too aware that it was the anti-apartheid film."

Mr. Jones brought a cassette of the 1951 version with him to study, and said he admired Canada Lee's performance of Stephen Kumalo as "a stalwart oak." His own Stephen Kumalo, he said, would be less oaklike, perhaps more Christlike in his almost dogmatic insistence on turning the other cheek.

"Young people will probably feel more comfortable with Canada's than mine," Mr. Jones said. "There's something very unsettling about someone who insists on turning the other cheek. Because we're all afraid we won't survive that way."

"Lost in the Stars," the 1949 stage adaptation by Maxwell Anderson with music by Kurt Weill, was a critical triumph, although Mr. Paton loathed everything about it but the music.

His biographer, Mr. Alexander, suggests that Mr. Paton, who was religious and hopeful, found the Broadway version too agnostic and bleak. The subtitle of *Cry, the Beloved Country*, after all, is "A Story of Comfort in Desolation." "Lost in the Stars" found little cause for comfort.

The new version aspires to be more faithful to the author's intent, and to his prose. Much of the incantatory narrative, biblical in its cadence and evocative of rural Africa, is voiced over in Mr. Jones's familiar baritone, with what he calls "my attempted Zulu accent."

The production was filmed on South African locations that are drenched in history.

One night Winnie Mandela, the estranged wife of Nelson Mandela, dropped by to watch Mr. Jones, as the country parson, arrive bewildered in a Pretoria square transformed by period street lights and vintage buses into 1940's Johannesburg.

The backdrop was the Palace of Justice where in 1964 Mrs. Mandela watched her husband being sentenced to life imprisonment. The trial of Stephen Kumalo's son, Absalom, was filmed in courtroom C, where Mr. Mandela was tried.

Aside from three leading players—Mr. Jones, Richard Harris as the father of the murdered white man and Charles Dutton as Stephen Kumalo's brother, a duplicitous firebrand—the cast and crew are South Africans.

The screenwriter, Ronald Harwood, who was an Oscar nominee for *The Dresser*, is South African-born.

Anant Singh, the South African producer, said he bought the rights to the novel six years ago, planning to hoard the story until he could make it as a celebration of the country's freedom.

"Of course, Paton never imagined that it could ever happen in this century," he said.

Social Issues in Literature

CHAPTER 3

Contemporary Perspectives on Race Relations in South Africa

Reconciliation Is the Path to Democracy in South Africa

Nelson Mandela

Nelson Mandela was the first president of South Africa to be elected in a fully representative election. An antiapartheid activist, he spent twenty-seven years in prison for his political activities. Upon his release, Mandela adopted a policy of reconciliation that led to a multiracial democracy in South Africa. With Frederik Willem de Klerk, the last president of apartheid-era South Africa, he won the Nobel Peace Prize in 1993.

In the following viewpoint, a condensed version of the original speech, Nelson Mandela argues that the path to freedom begins and ends with reconciliation. Central to the process of reconciliation in South Africa is the Truth and Reconciliation Commission, which uncovered crimes during the apartheid era and had the power to grant amnesty to those who confessed. Mandela contends that it is important to recall the past, with all of its injustices, so that South Africa can ensure that such inhumanity never again occurs.

The experience of others has taught us that nations that do not deal with the past are haunted by it for generations. The quest for reconciliation was the fundamental objective of our struggle to set up a government based on the will of the people and to build a South Africa that indeed belongs to all. The quest for reconciliation was the spur that gave impetus to our difficult negotiation process and the agreements that emerged from it.

Nelson Mandela, Excerpt from "Opening address by President Nelson Mandela in the special debate on the report of the Truth and Reconciliation Commission" at the Parliament, Cape Town, South Africa, February 25, 1999. Nelson Mandela Foundation (co-listing ANC Website, NMS672, June/July 1999). Copyright © 1999 Nelson Mandela. Reproduced by permission.

A Nation at Peace with Itself

The desire to attain a nation at peace with itself and able to build a better life for all is the primary motivation for our Reconstruction and Development Programme. The Truth and Reconciliation Commission, which operated from 1995 to 1998, was an important component of that process. The group uncovered crimes committed during the apartheid era and could choose to provide amnesty to those who confessed. Its work was a critical milestone in a journey that has just started. Political and business leaders, along with those in the trade union movement, religious bodies, and the communities, must remain focused on the matters that the Commission brought to the fore.

The path toward reconciliation touches upon every facet of our lives. Reconciliation requires the dismantling of apartheid and the measures that reinforced it. It requires that we overcome the consequences of that inhuman system that live on in our attitudes toward one another as well as in the poverty and inequality that affect the lives of millions.

Just as we reached out across the divisions of centuries to establish democracy, we need now to work together in all our diversity, including the variety of our experiences and recollections of our history, to overcome the divisions themselves and eradicate their consequences. Reconciliation is central to the vision that moved millions of men and women to risk all, including their lives, in the struggle against apartheid and white domination. It is inseparable from the achievement of a nonracial, democratic, and united nation that affords common citizenship, rights, and obligations to each and every person, while it respects the rich diversity of our people.

We think of those whom apartheid sought to imprison in the jails of hate and fear. We think, too, of those it infused with a false sense of superiority to justify their inhumanity to others, as well as those it conscripted into the machines of destruction, exacting a heavy toll among them in life and limb

Thomas Ndobe in a luxury room of The Outpost Lodge in Kruger National Park on September 13, 2003. The Makuleke people won the land back after being forcibly removed by the former apartheid regime. They won it in a 1998 settlement with the South African democratic government. AP Images.

and giving them a warped disregard for life. We think of the millions of South Africans who still live in poverty because of apartheid, disadvantaged and excluded from opportunity by the discrimination of the past.

Recalling the Past

We recall our terrible past so that we can deal with it, forgiving where forgiveness is necessary—but not forgetting. By remembering, we can ensure that never again will such inhumanity tear us apart, and we can eradicate a dangerous legacy that still lurks as a threat to our democracy.

It was inevitable that a task of such magnitude, begun so recently and requiring a process that will take many years to complete, would suffer various limitations. Its ultimate success will depend on all sectors of our society recognizing with the world that apartheid was a crime against humanity and that its vile deeds transcended our borders and sowed the seeds of destruction—producing a harvest that we reap even today. About this there can be no equivocation: Recognizing apartheid's evil lies at the heart of the new constitution of our democracy.

We should draw pride from the new constitution and from the openness and accountability that have become trademarks of our society. And we should recommit ourselves to these values and to practical action that promotes our view that a strong human-rights culture is rooted in the material conditions of our lives. None of us can enjoy lasting peace and security while a part of our nation lives in poverty.

We should not underestimate the difficulties of integrating into our society those who have committed gross violations of human rights and those convicted of being informers and collaborators. But we also have many encouraging examples of great generosity and nobility on the part of our community members. Their deeds are a reproach to those who sought amnesty without remorse and an inspiration to others pursuing the difficult, sensitive task of reintegration.

The best reparation for the suffering of victims and communities—and the highest recognition of their efforts—is the transformation of our society into one that makes a living reality of the human rights for which they struggled. We should forgive but not forget. Leaders should emerge from all parties and all walks of life to build our nation. Its foundation will be hope and its edifice a future that we create together.

Racial Reconciliation in South Africa Is Not Complete

Desmond Tutu

Desmond Tutu is a South African political activist and the Anglican archbishop emeritus of Cape Town who was a vocal opponent of apartheid. He chaired the Truth and Reconciliation Commission following the end of apartheid and won the Nobel Peace Prize in 1984.

In this 2003 interview with Maclean's *magazine, Desmond Tutu states that although much has been accomplished in the ten years since the end of apartheid in South Africa, there is still a great deal to accomplish to improve race relations in that country. He finds leadership to be the biggest challenge facing all of Africa, and he is critical of governments that have not been accountable to their people. Tutu's faith gives him hope for the future of Africa, and he believes that good will eventually prevail.*

Archbishop Desmond Tutu . . . is an icon of the anti-apartheid struggle. Throughout his life he has been an unwavering and irrepressible voice for the oppressed. His moral authority is matched only by that of Nelson Mandela, a fellow Nobel Peace Prize laureate. As the former chairman of South Africa's Truth and Reconciliation Commission, his name is synonymous with the difficult and contentious effort to heal the wounds of apartheid-era human rights abuses. Despite retirement and a battle with prostate cancer, "The Arch," as he is affectionately known, is still a close observer of African politics. He spoke with *Maclean's* Johannesburg correspondent Alan Martin about the challenges the continent faces.

Desmond Tutu, "Power Tends to Corrupt," *Maclean's*, vol. 116, no. 46, November 17, 2003, pp. 110, 114. Copyright © Rogers Publishing Limited 2003. Reproduced by permission of the author.

Faith Gives Hope for Africa

Alan Martin: What gives you hope for Africa?

Desmond Tutu: Because it's God's world and ultimately God is in charge, and good will prevail. Sometimes the objective facts might appear to contradict that. When you think that we have had slavery that devastated this continent, colonialism and the aftermath of that, being involved as surrogates in the Cold War—all of those things would make one wonder if there is hope. We have had wars of all kinds, genocide, and conflicts, such as in Angola, that were the machinations of superpowers. Yet Africa has emerged from the shackles of slavery and colonialism. Apartheid has ended and the most admired human being in the world is an African—Nelson Mandela. We have amazed the world by the nature of the transition that has happened here.

The West tends to blame many of the continent's problems on Africans themselves, suggesting they are incapable of running modern democracies.

I'm always intrigued by Westerners who show an incredible lack of knowledge of their own history. They forget how long it took them to move to a situation of relative security. They forget that Nazism, Communism and Fascism are Western inventions. They forget that no other nation has dropped an atom bomb on another nation except Westerners. They seem to forget the Holocaust was engineered by Westerners, that two so-called world wars were brought about by Westerners. One wishes they would have a modicum of modesty and not seek to arrogantly pass judgment on others who are experiencing the travails associated with the evolution of democracy.

Leadership Is Biggest Challenge

What's the biggest challenge facing Africa?

We face a very serious crisis of leadership and are falling short in matters of good governance. We have had our fair share of governments that are not accountable to people—

leaders who tended to think that power accruing to them is for their own self-aggrandizement. That makes it more difficult to face up to the quite daunting challenges before us— poverty, disease. These are challenges that could more easily be dealt with if we had governments that responded to the wishes of the governed.

How satisfied are you with the way South African President Thabo Mbeki has handled the crisis in Zimbabwe?

There did seem to be a time when quiet diplomacy was bringing about results. But I am aware of the constraints under which Mbeki operates. One of them is a very serious one. Until Mandela came out of prison, every camera, every journalist, used to hang on [Zimbabwean president Robert] Mugabe's lips. Mbeki is younger. There is resentment that he is being an upstart. I've been saddened that fundamental human rights are being violated. I would have hoped we would have been able to say to Mugabe, "We understand the problems you are having, but we cannot accept what you are doing."

The West has been reluctant to get involved in African conflicts—whether it be the Rwandan genocide, the war in the Democratic Republic of Congo, or more recently Liberia. Is there a racist overtone to this?

Don't you think so? There are lives that are more valuable than others. Look at the coverage of the casualties in Iraq. How many people have died? Thousands. And yet the way the media portrays that, you get way more coverage for the one American soldier that gets killed. What about the umpteen innocent, defenceless Iraqi civilians? I hope that one day the world will come to realize that we all count equally before God.

Reconciliation Is a Process

In South Africa, many notorious killers, including those of Steve Biko, were granted amnesty by the Truth and Reconciliation Commission. How do you feel when some of the worst offenders walked free?

What riles people is that you wish you could see an answering generosity from whites that responds to the generosity from the victims. Instead there was a lot of hairsplitting. And I'm sad, sad, sad, that on the whole these people have not engaged in the business of transformation or understood that we have to do all we can to change the physical circumstances of most of our black citizens. But even now, you have people who are acquitted in courts and take that to mean they are innocent.

Why are African leaders so reluctant to criticize their own, for example Mugabe?

Part of it is that you are perceived to be a lackey of the West. I feel they could have been a great deal more forthright with Mugabe, saying, "We understand you have a problem of land distribution, but you don't solve that by behaving in a way that violates all sorts of rights and subverts the law." It's profoundly wrong, and we don't equivocate.

How satisfied are you with the present state of race relations in South Africa?

It's extraordinary what we have accomplished in 10 years. But do we have reconciliation? No. Reconciliation is not something you accomplish overnight. It's a process. Each one of us has to make a contribution. It's a national project. Sometimes I think we have become blasé at what we have achieved. But there is still a great deal to do. The legacy of apartheid is horrendous.

Several African countries emerging from dictatorships or war have begun or are toying with the idea of truth commissions modelled on South Africa's example. What advice would you offer them?

The basic principles perhaps apply universally, but they must ensure whatever process they put in place will be something that has come about as a result of as wide a participation of society as possible.

What do you think will happen after your generation has passed on?

The younger leaders are going to have to face up to other challenges that will test their mettle. It will be other kinds of challenges, like the temptations of power. As you know, power tends to corrupt and absolute power tends to corrupt absolutely. We are not exempt from that. We had other challenges. They are going to have to discover for themselves what the raison d'être of leadership is. Why am I a leader? It is a question that each one of them is going to have to ask.

A History of Racial Conflict Continues in South Africa

Marco MacFarlane

Marco MacFarlane is the head of research at the South African Institute of Race Relations in Johannesburg.

In the following viewpoint, Marco MacFarlane argues that the current wave of interracial violence in South Africa has its roots in a history of cultural and racial conflict. He faults the government for adopting policies that encourage competition between races, rather than promoting interracial forgiveness and harmony.

The vast majority of South African history is one of division, both cultural and racial, and it seems that that history is shaping the events of today. Blacks fought whites, Zulus fought Xhosas, Boers fought the English. On every level, both between and within every cultural grouping, South Africans have been taught to fight each other by our fathers and their fathers before them. The xenophobic attacks that have thrown our country into turmoil serve as a bitter reminder that our history of inter-racial and inter-cultural conflict continues to harm our nation to this day.

A Culture of Blame

For some years there have been widespread protests in poor communities over service delivery. To many in these communities, it has increasingly felt as if their pleas have fallen on deaf ears, and that the government will never take notice of their suffering. Policy failures and lack of communication

Marco MacFarlane, "Will We Ever Be Able to Live with Each Other?" *SAIRR Today*, May 23, 2008. Copyright © 2008 South African Institute of Race Relations. Reproduced by permission.

from the government have allowed these grievances to fester, but none of these frustrations can find an outlet when dealing with the highest bureaucracy in the land. Foreigners, however, are close at hand. They are an easy target, they are offered only minimal protection in our legal system, and, best of all, they are easy to blame and even easier to punish.

This culture of blame and retribution can only lead to social and economic disaster, and it has done so time and again throughout Africa and indeed the world. The problem is compounded by the fact that blame can indeed be apportioned for the current circumstances of the poor and downtrodden in South Africa. We can blame generations of colonialism, apartheid, racial discrimination and institutionalised injustice. But these causes cannot be punished. They cannot be reprimanded or altered, and the results remain long after the perpetrators have gone to their graves. There is little satisfaction to be gained by condemning our past, but it should not escape our notice that continued inter-cultural hatred condemns our future as well.

Government Racially Divisive

Our government has done little to foster inter-cultural forgiveness and understanding, for the thrust of government policy implies that inter-cultural or inter-racial competition is at the very heart of South African life. Our policy-makers are determined to redistribute land from white farmers to black ones, in business our hiring policies are structured on explicitly racial grounds, and the highest levels of our economy are governed by black economic empowerment and similar race-based laws. The policy environment is one that accepts the fallacy that there are limited resources, and that cultures and races need to compete for these resources. In South Africa we have an environment where the vast majority of our resources remain untapped and unutilised. We have a workforce that is large and underemployed, but we have failed to train them.

White laborers harvest melons on a farm in Orania, South Africa on February 10, 2004. Some 600 Afrikaners are building their dream of an ethnically pure homeland on the edge of the Karoo Desert. Black laborers that once symbolized white privilege, are not allowed. AP Images.

We have well established infrastructure that is sufficient only for some, but we insist on redistributing ownership of that insufficiency rather than building more capacity. We have a nation that is desperate to heal the wounds that have been inflicted on us for generations, but we have compounded the injury by framing all of our arguments in the terms of the oppressors. We are a nation divided and dividing, as factions replace families and foreigners replace friends.

We have been taught to blame one another. We fail to see each other as people, rather we find it easier to dehumanise one another and put each other into categories of culpability. Our neighbours are not people; they are part of a monolithic faceless group that is the source of all our woes. We are not maiming and burning human beings, we are punishing perpetrators. We are administering justice.

The irony is that race and culture are only illusions. They serve as proxies for social status and economic power. They are arbitrary groupings that we assign to ourselves and to others so that we can simultaneously assign value. For a racist white person, all the negative aspects in our country can be assigned to the blacks. For a xenophobic black person it will be foreigners that are to blame for social ills. It is a quick and easy way of saying who is bad or good, since those values are seen to depend not on an individual but on group membership.

History has taught us the danger of these methods of thought, and the current violence sweeping parts of the country serves as a powerful example of it. Perhaps one day, South Africans will discover that our strength flows from our unity and our humanity, not from the colour of our skins or the languages we speak. It is with infinite sadness that we must acknowledge that that day is not today.

Racial Conflict Still Haunts Postapartheid South Africa

Joshua Hammer

Joshua Hammer was Newsweek's *bureau chief in Cape Town for two years, living in the city until April 2007. He is currently a freelance writer based in Berlin.*

In the following viewpoint, Joshua Hammer describes a complex and shifting racial situation in Cape Town and suggests that the legacy of apartheid still lingers in South Africa. While Cape Town is a prosperous and growing city, the unemployment rate is 50 percent and the AIDS rate is high. Hammer explains that the greatest conflict in Cape Town is between blacks and those of mixed race—blacks resent those of mixed race for not supporting the African National Congress and those of mixed race fear black competition for jobs. Reactions to power failures are an example of tension under the surface; these failures are used as evidence that the blacks in power are unqualified for their jobs. Hammer concludes that these are natural steps in the path toward democracy.

From the deck of a 40-foot sloop plying the chilly waters of Table Bay, Paul Maré gazes back at the illuminated skyline of Cape Town. It is early evening, at the close of a clear day in December. Maré and his crew, racing in the Royal Cape Yacht Club's final regatta before Christmas, hoist the jib and head the sloop out to sea. A fierce southeaster is blowing, typical of this time of year, and Maré's crew members cheer as they tack round the last race buoy and speed back toward shore and a celebratory braai, or barbecue, awaiting them on the club's patio.

Maré, the descendant of French Huguenots who immigrated to South Africa in the late 17th century, is president of the yacht club, one of many white colonial vestiges that still thrive in Cape Town—South Africa's "Mother City." The club, founded in 1904 after the Second Boer War, has drawn an almost exclusively white membership ever since. (Today, however, the club administers the Sail Training Academy, which provides instruction to disadvantaged youth, most of them blacks and coloureds.)

After Nelson Mandela's African National Congress (ANC) won power in South Africa in the democratic elections of 1994 (it has governed since), some of Maré's white friends left the country, fearing that it would suffer the economic decline, corruption and violence that befell other post-independence African nations. Maré's two grown children immigrated to London, but the 69-year-old engineering consultant does not regret remaining in the land of his birth. His life in suburban Newlands, one of the affluent enclaves on the verdant slopes of Table Mountain, is stable and comfortable. His leisure time is centered around his yacht, which he owns with a fellow white South African. "We'll be getting ready for our next crossing soon," says Maré, who has sailed three times across the often stormy south Atlantic.

A State of Transition

More than a decade after the end of apartheid, Cape Town, founded in 1652 by the Dutch East India Company's Jan van Riebeeck, is one of the fastest-growing cities in the country. Much of this sprawling metropolis of 3.3 million people at Africa's southern tip has the feel of a European or American playground, a hybrid of Wyoming's Tetons, California's Big Sur and the Provence region of France. White Capetonians enjoy a quality of life that most Europeans would envy— surfing and sailing off some of the world's most beautiful beaches, tasting wine at vineyards established more than 300 years ago by South Africa's first Dutch settlers, and mountain biking on wilderness trails high above the sea. Cape Town is the only major city in South Africa whose mayor is white, and whites still control most of its businesses. Not surprisingly, it's still known as "the most European city in South Africa."

But a closer look reveals a city in the throes of transformation. Downtown Cape Town, where one saw relatively few black faces in the early 1990s (the apartheid government's pass laws excluded nearly all black Africans from the Western Cape province), bustles with African markets. Each day at a central bus depot, combis, or minibuses, deposit immigrants by the hundreds from as far away as Nigeria and Senegal, nearly all of them seeking jobs. The ANC's "black economic empowerment" initiatives have elevated thousands of previously disadvantaged Africans to the middle class and created a new generation of black and mixed-race millionaires and even billionaires. With the racial hierarchy dictated by apartheid outlawed, the city has become a noisy mix of competing constituencies and ethnicities—all jockeying for a share of power. The post-apartheid boom has also seen spiraling crime in black townships and white suburbs, a high rate of HIV infection and a housing shortage that has forced tens of thousands of destitute black immigrants to live in dangerous squatter camps.

Now Cape Town has begun preparing for what will be the city's highest-profile event since the end of white-minority rule in 1994. In 2004, the world soccer federation, FIFA, selected South Africa as the venue for the 2010 World Cup. Preparations include construction of a $300 million, 68,000-seat showcase stadium in the prosperous Green Point neighborhood along the Atlantic Ocean and massive investment in infrastructure. Not surprisingly, the project has generated a controversy tinged with racial overtones. A group of affluent whites, who insist that the stadium will lose money and degrade the environment, has been pitted against black leaders convinced that opponents want to prevent black soccer fans from flooding into their neighborhood. The controversy has abated thanks to a promise by the Western Cape government, so far unfulfilled, to build an urban park next to the stadium. "For Capetonians, the World Cup is more than just a football match," says Shaun Johnson, a former executive of a newspaper group and a top aide to former President [Nelson] Mandela. "It's an opportunity to show ourselves off to the world."

Reminders of Apartheid

For nearly two years, from August 2005 until April 2007, I experienced Cape Town's often surreal contradictions firsthand. I lived just off a winding country road high in the Steenberg Mountains, bordering Table Mountain National Park and overlooking False Bay, 12 miles south of Cape Town's city center. From my perch, it was easy to forget that I was living in Africa. Directly across the road from my house sprawled the Tokai forest, where I jogged or mountain-biked most mornings through dense groves of pine and eucalyptus planted by Cape Town's English colonial masters nearly a century ago. A half mile from my house, an 18th-century vineyard boasted three gourmet restaurants and a lily-white clientele; it could have been plucked whole from the French countryside.

Yet there were regular reminders of the legacy of apartheid. When I drove my son down the mountain to the American International School each morning, I passed a parade of black workers from the townships in the Cape Flats trudging uphill to manicure the gardens and clean the houses of my white neighbors. Next to my local shopping mall, and across the road from a golf course used almost exclusively by whites, stood an even starker reminder of South Africa's recent past: Pollsmoor Prison, where Mandela spent four and a half years after being moved from Robben Island in April 1984.

I also lived within sight of Table Mountain, the sandstone and granite massif that stands as the iconic image of the city.

Formed 60 million years ago, when rock burst through the earth's surface during the violent tectonic split of Africa from South America, the 3,563-foot peak once rose as high as 19,500-foot Mount Kilimanjaro. No other place in Cape Town better symbolizes the city's grand scale, embrace of outdoor life and changing face. Table Mountain National Park—the preserve that Cecil Rhodes, prime minister of the Cape Colony in the late 19th century, carved out of private farms on the slopes of the mountain—has grown into a 60,000-acre contiguous wilderness, extending from the heart of the city to the southern tip of the Cape Peninsula; it includes dozens of miles of coastline. The park is a place of astonishing biodiversity; 8,500 varieties of bush-like flora, or fynbos—all unique to the Western Cape—cover the area, along with wildlife as varied as mountain goats, tortoises, springboks and baboons.

One December day I drive up to the park's rustic headquarters to meet Paddy Gordon, 44, area manager of the park section that lies within metropolitan Cape Town. Gordon exemplifies the changes that have taken place in the country over the past decade or so: a mixed-race science graduate of the once-segregated University of the Western Cape, he became, in 1989, the first nonwhite appointed to a managerial job in the entire national park system. Within 12 years he had worked his way up to the top job. "Before I came along we were only laborers," he says. . . .

A Changing Economy

During the height of anti-apartheid protests in the 1970s and 1980s, Cape Town, geographically isolated and insulated from racial strife by the near absence of a black population, remained quiet in comparison with Johannesburg's seething townships. Then, during the dying days of apartheid, blacks began to pour into Cape Town—as many as 50,000 a year over the past decade. In the 1994 election campaign, the white-dominated National Party exploited coloureds' fear that a black-led government would give their jobs to blacks; most chose the National Party over the ANC. While many blacks resent mixed-race Capetonians for their failure to embrace the ANC, many coloureds still fear black competition for government grants and jobs. "The divide between blacks and coloureds is the real racial fault line in Cape Town," I was told by Henry Jeffreys, a Johannesburg resident who moved to Cape Town [in 2007] to become the first nonwhite editor of the newspaper *Die Burger*. (A former editor was the architect of apartheid, D.F. Malan.)

But the gap is closing. The Western Cape province, of which Cape Town is the heart, boasts one of the fastest-growing economies in South Africa. An infusion of foreign and local investment has transformed the once moribund city center into what civic leader Shaun Johnson calls a "forest of cranes." In late 2006, a Dubai consortium paid more than $1 billion for the Victoria and Alfred Waterfront, a complex of hotels, restaurants and shops—and the terminal for ferries that transport tourists across Table Bay to Robben Island. The price of real estate has skyrocketed, even in once-rundown seaside neighborhoods such as Mouille Point, and the bubble shows no signs of bursting.

The new economic activity is enriching South Africans who couldn't dream of sharing in the wealth not that long ago. One bright morning, I drive south along the slopes of Table Mountain to Constantia Valley, a lush expanse of villas and vineyards; its leafy byways epitomize the privileged lives of Cape Town's white elite—the horsey "mink and manure set." I have come to meet Ragavan Moonsamy, 43, or "Ragi," as he prefers to be called, one of South Africa's newest multi-millionaires.

Here, bougainvillea-shrouded mansions lie hidden behind high walls; horse trails wind up forested hills cloaked in chestnut, birch, pine and eucalyptus. Armed "rapid response" security teams patrol the quiet lanes. I drive through the electric gates of a three-acre estate, passing landscaped gardens before I pull up in front of a neocolonial mansion, parking beside a Bentley, two Porsches and a Lamborghini Spyder. Moonsamy, wearing jeans and a T-shirt is waiting for me at the door.

As recently as 15 years ago, the only way that Moonsamy would have gained entrance to this neighborhood would have been as a gardener or laborer. He grew up with eight siblings in a two-room house in Athlone, a dreary township in the Cape Flats. His great-grandparents had come to the South African port of Durban from southern India to work the sugarcane fields as indentured servants in the late 19th century. Moonsamy's parents moved illegally from Durban to Cape Town in the 1940s. He says he and his siblings "saw Table Mountain every day, but we were indoctrinated by apartheid to believe we do not belong there. From the time I was a young teenager, I knew I wanted to get out."

After graduating from a segregated high school, Moonsamy dabbled in anti-apartheid activism. In 1995, as the ANC government began seeking ways of propelling "previously disadvantaged" people into the mainstream economy, Moonsamy started his own finance company, UniPalm Investments. He organized thousands of black and mixed-race investors to buy shares in large companies such as a subsidiary of Telkom, South Africa's state-owned phone monopoly, and bought significant stakes in them himself. Over ten years, Moonsamy has put together billions of dollars in deals, made tens of millions for himself and, in 1996, purchased this property in the most exclusive corner of Upper Constantia, one of the first non-whites to do so. He says he's just getting started. "Ninety-five percent of this economy is still white-owned, and changing the ownership will take a long time," he told me. Speaking figuratively, he adds that the city is the place to seize opportunity: "If you want to catch a marlin, you've got to come to Cape Town."

Complex Racial Dynamics

Not everybody catches marlin. Zongeswa Bauli, 39, is a loyal member of the ANC who wears Nelson Mandela T-shirts and has voted for the party in every election since 1994. One afternoon I travel with her to her home at the Kanana squatter camp, an illegal settlement inside the black township of Guguletu, near Cape Town's airport. In 1991, the dying days of apartheid, Bauli arrived here from destitute Ciskei—one of the so-called "independent black homelands" set up by the apartheid regime in the 1970s—in what is now Eastern Cape province. For nine years, she camped in her grandmother's backyard and worked as a domestic servant for white families. In 2000, she purchased a plot for a few hundred dollars in Kanana, now home to 6,000 black migrants—and growing by 10 percent annually.

Bauli leads me through sandy alleys, past shacks constructed of crudely nailed wood planks. Mosquitoes swarm over pools of stagnant water. In the courtyard of a long-abandoned student hostel now taken over by squatters, rats scurry around heaps of rotting garbage; residents tell me that someone dumped a body here a month ago, and it lay undiscovered for several days. While free anti-retroviral drugs have been introduced in Cape Town, the HIV rate remains high, and the unemployment rate is more than 50 percent; every male we meet, it seems, is jobless, and though it's only 5 p.m., most appear drunk. As we near her dwelling, Bauli points out a broken outdoor water pump, vandalized the week before. At last we arrive at her tiny wooden shack, divided into three cubicles, where she lives with her 7-year-old daughter, Sisipho, her sister and her sister's three children. (After years of agitation by squatters, the municipality agreed in 2001 to provide electricity to the camp. Bauli has it, but thousands of more recent arrivals do not.) After dark, she huddles with her family indoors, the flimsy door locked, terrified of the gangsters, called tsotsis, who control the camp at night. "It's too dangerous out there," she says.

Bauli dreams of escaping Kanana. The ANC has promised to provide new housing for all of Cape Town's squatters before the World Cup begins—the "No Shacks 2010" pledge—but Bauli has heard such talk before. "Nobody cares about Guguletu," she says with a shrug. Bauli's hopes rest on her daughter who is in second grade in a public primary school in the affluent, largely white neighborhood of Kenilworth—an unattainable aspiration in the apartheid era. "Maybe by 2020, Sisipho will be able to buy me a house," she says wryly.

Helen Zille, Cape Town's mayor, largely blames the ANC for the housing crisis: the $50 million that Cape Town receives annually from the national government, she says, is barely enough to build houses for 7,000 families. "The waiting list is growing by 20,000 [families] a year," she told me.

Zille's own story reflects the city's complex racial dynamics. In the last local election, her Democratic Alliance (DA), a white-dominated opposition party, formed a coalition with half a dozen smaller parties to defeat the incumbent ANC. (Many coloured voters turned against the ANC once again and helped give the DA its victory.) It was one of the first times in South Africa since the end of apartheid that the ANC had been turned out of office; the election results created a backlash that still resonates.

Zille, 57, is one of only a few white politicians in the country who speak Xhosa, the language of South Africa's second-largest tribe, and lives in a racially integrated neighborhood. She has an impressive record as an activist, having been arrested during the apartheid years for her work as a teacher in Crossroads, a black squatter camp. Despite her credentials, the ANC-controlled Western Cape provincial government launched an effort [in the fall of 2007] to unseat and replace her with a "mayoral committee" heavily represented by

ANC members. Their complaint: the city was not "African" enough and had to be brought in line with the rest of the country. After protests from Zille supporters and criticism from even some ANC allies, the leadership backed down.

The wounds are still raw. Zille bristled when I asked her about being heckled at a rally she attended with South African President Thabo Mbeki. She said the heckling was "orchestrated" by her enemies within the ANC. "This election marked the first time that the party of liberation has lost anywhere in South Africa," she said as we sat in her spacious sixth-floor office in the Civic Center, a high-rise overlooking Cape Town's harbor. "The ANC didn't like that." As for the claim that Cape Town wasn't African enough, she scoffed. "Rubbish! Are they saying that only Xhosa people can be considered African? The tragedy is that the ANC has fostered the misimpression that only black people can take care of blacks."

ANC Blamed for Power Crisis

The Koeberg Nuclear Power Station, Africa's only nuclear power plant, was inaugurated in 1984 by the apartheid regime and is the major source of electricity for the Western Cape's 4.5 million population. I've come to meet Carin De Villiers, a senior manager for Eskom, South Africa's power monopoly. De Villiers was an eyewitness to one of the worst crises in South Africa's recent history, which unfolded at Koeberg for two frantic weeks in early 2006. It may well have contributed to the defeat of the ANC in the last election.

On February 19, 2006, an overload on a high-voltage transmission line automatically tripped the nuclear reactor's single working unit (the other had earlier sustained massive damage after a worker dropped a three-inch bolt into a water pump). With the entire reactor suddenly out of commission, the whole Western Cape became dependent on a coal-fueled plant located more than 1,000 miles away. As engineers tried desperately to get one of the two 900-megawatt units back on line,

Eskom ordered rolling blackouts that paralyzed Cape Town and the region, as far as Namibia, for two weeks. "It was a nightmare," De Villiers told me. Businesses shut down, traffic lights stopped working, gas pumps and ATMs went dead. Police-stations, medical clinics and government offices had to operate by candlelight. After the city's pumps shut down, raw sewage poured into rivers and wetlands, killing thousands of fish and threatening the Cape Peninsula's rich bird life. Tourists were stranded in cable cars on Table Mountain; burglars took advantage of disabled alarms to wreak havoc in affluent neighborhoods. By the time Eskom restored power on March 3, the blackouts had cost the economy hundreds of millions of dollars.

For De Villiers and the rest of Cape Town's population, the power failures provided an unsettling look at the fragility that lies just beneath the city's prosperous surface. It drew attention to the fact that Eskom has failed to expand power capacity to keep up with the province's 6 percent annual growth and opened the ANC to charges of poor planning and bad management. Now Eskom is scrambling to build new plants, including another nuclear reactor, as the city prepares for the World Cup. The power collapse also laid bare racial grievances: many whites, and some nonwhites as well, saw the breakdown as evidence that the official policy of black economic empowerment had brought unqualified people into key positions of responsibility. "Given the mismanagement of this economy à la Eskom, I am beginning to prefer my oppressors to be white," one reader wrote to *Business Day*, a South African newspaper.

Paul Maré considers such rough patches a natural, if frustrating, part of the transition to real democracy. Standing on the deck of the Royal Cape Yacht Club at twilight, with a glass of South African chardonnay in one hand and a boerewors (grilled sausage) in the other. Maré takes in the glittering lights of downtown Cape Town and the scene of prosperous white South Africa that surrounds him. Maré's partner, Lindsay Birch, 67, grumbles that in the post-apartheid era, "it's hard for us to get sponsorship for our regattas. Sailing isn't a black sport." Maré, however, is putting his bets on Cape Town's future—and his place in it. "I'm an African," Maré says. "I've got 350 years' worth of history behind me."

Racial Tensions Obscure the Real Issues in Postapartheid South Africa

The Economist

The Economist is a weekly global newspaper that focuses on current events in business and politics. Its articles are anonymous because the paper believes content to be more important than authors.

In this article that appeared in The Economist, *the authors suggest that race may not be as important an issue in South Africa as is popularly believed. Joblessness, crime, and the spread of HIV are considered more fundamental problems. They argue that race is often used as an excuse for some of these fundamental problems. The African National Congress government is guilty of exacerbating racial tensions in its efforts to redirect contracts to the "previously disadvantaged." The authors recommend that income rather than race be used to define a disadvantaged status.*

On the face of it, race still permeates everything in South Africa. Take television. A show called *Idols*, which grooms wannabe pop stars, got into trouble when a black judge criticised a white contestant using a Zulu expression that the contestant did not understand. Irate fans accused the judge of being a racist. More recently, a black model voted out of the *Strictly Come Dancing* show, in which celebrities display their dubious ballroom-dancing talents, unleashed accusations of racism when she complained that her "own people" did not vote for her.

"Shades of Black," *The Economist*, vol. 380, no. 8494, September 9, 2006, pp 48–49. Copyright © 2006 The Economist Newspaper Limited, London. Republished with permission of The Economist Newspaper Group, conveyed through Copyright Clearance Center, Inc.

At the other end of the spectrum, whites are often accused of resisting change. Yet there is also increasing evidence despite the lingering sensitivities that, 12 years after the end of apartheid, race may not be as important as it seems. According to a recent survey, 60% of South Africans believe that race relations are actually improving. Even more strikingly, when Markinor, a polling company, asked people about the most important problems that the government should tackle, joblessness, crime and HIV/AIDS topped the list; racism and affirmative action did not even appear. This suggests that the faultlines may be changing within South African politics and that, insofar as race does come up, it is often used as a proxy for other problems, such as poverty or frustration over the slow pace at which wealth is being redistributed.

Ironically, however, some fear that it is now African National Congress (ANC) politicians in government, stout opponents of apartheid that they were, who are doing as much as anyone to perpetuate the very apartheid-era classifications that the country is trying to move beyond. Take the party's flagship policy to try and redress the gross economic inequalities inherited from apartheid, the black economic empowerment programme. Companies that expect to get even minor contracts from the government have to include more of the "previously disadvantaged", understood to mean primarily blacks, Indians and coloureds (as mixed-race people are still known), among their shareholders and employees, as well as in their boardrooms.

The policy has been criticised for creating costly distortions rather than new jobs and for lining the pockets of a small elite of well-connected bankers and lawyers. Allan Boesak, a former chairman of the Western Cape's ANC branch, laments that the ruling party has brought back the language of racial division, a claim often made by the Democratic Alliance, an opposition party.

South African police check the scene of a burning shack in the Reiger Park informal settlement near Johannesburg in May 2008. Clashes between the poor have caused 22 deaths and focused attention on the complaints that South Africa's post-apartheid government has failed to deliver. AP Images.

A recent court ruling confirming a decision by Eskom, the country's main electricity company, to favour a black applicant over a more experienced coloured employee for a job, on the grounds that he was more disadvantaged under the previous regime, has also raised tensions. Such incidents feed the suspicion among some coloureds that they have gone from being not white enough under apartheid to being not black enough today. Coloured residents of Ravensmead, a Cape Town township, protested last year against the city's plans to build houses for the black dwellers of a squatter camp that burnt down, saying that they had been there longer and should be first in line.

Two years ago the media adviser to the former ANC mayor of Cape Town argued on his website that blacks were superior to coloureds, who risk dying "of a drunken death". He was eventually fired, but the incident created ill-feeling. The battle over the ANC leadership in the Western Cape province last year which Ebrahim Rasool, the coloured premier, lost to James Ngculu, raised questions over whether race had been a factor in the result.

Rising immigration also complicates the picture. Since the end of apartheid, the continent's richest country has been a magnet for Africans fleeing war, persecution or poverty. Some 3m refugees from Zimbabwe alone may now live in South Africa. Perceptions that foreigners are stealing jobs and fuelling crime have risen. A recent report from Human Rights Watch, an international lobby group, documents abuse of illegal Zimbabwean migrants not only by employers but also by the (mainly black) police. Somali shopkeepers have been targeted and shot.

The South African Institute of Race Relations, a think-tank, argues that race should no longer be a proxy for "disadvantage" and that this should instead be defined by income. In the long run, the ability of South Africans to get over their enduring tendency to think in colours will depend largely on making swathes of people less poor. Over 25% of the population (or up to 40%, depending on the definition) are unemployed, compared with 20% in 1994. Not surprisingly, the euphoria of the first few years of democracy has given way to mounting impatience.

Some of the country's politicians at times try to duck these and other issues by resorting to the lexicon of race. When Desmond Tutu, a Nobel Prize–winning former archbishop, questioned President Thabo Mbeki's leadership style, the latter accused him of being "an icon of the white people". The Democratic Alliance has also been accused of playing on racial tensions in the Western Cape to boost itself among the province's coloured people. Still, voters in general may be tiring of race as an electoral issue.

For Further Discussion

1. Jonathan Paton, the son of Alan Paton, writes that many of the views expressed by the character Arthur Jarvis in *Cry, the Beloved Country* were the views of his father. Based on the excerpts from Jonathan Paton's biography and that of Peter Alexander, what similarities in outlook do you see between Arthur Jarvis and Alan Paton?

2. Patrick Colm Hogan writes that racist beliefs need not involve race hatred and that in *Cry, the Beloved Country*, Paton has written a racist book. What does he mean by this? Do you agree or disagree with him? Why?

3. Harold R. Collins writes that *Cry, the Beloved Country* shows the effects of detribalization, when the old African customs were displaced by industrialism and nothing took their place. Can you think of some other examples of detribalization throughout history and in today's world? What happened and what were its effects?

4. Carol Iannone and Stephen Watson disagree in their readings of *Cry, the Beloved Country*. The former believes that Paton has a complex view of the forces of good and evil, while the latter believes that Paton offers simplistic answers. Do you agree with either critic? Give reasons to support your position.

5. Nelson Mandela writes that the path to freedom begins and ends in reconciliation. Do you think Alan Paton would agree with him? Give reasons for your opinion.

6. *The Economist* reports that black economic empowerment programs in South Africa have been responsible for creating greater racial tension. What might be the source of some of these tensions? Is this comparable to affirmative

action programs in the United States? What are the advantages and disadvantages of such programs? Are you in favor of them? Explain your answers.

For Further Reading

Andre Brink, *A Dry White Season*. London: W.H. Allen, 1979.

J.M. Coetzee, *Disgrace*. London: Secker and Warburg, 1999.

———, *The Life and Times of Michael K*. New York: Viking, 1984.

———, *Waiting for the Barbarians*. London: Secker and Warburg, 1980.

Bryce Courtney, *The Power of One*. New York: Random House, 1989.

Alexandra Fuller, *Don't Let's Go to the Dogs Tonight: An African Childhood*. New York: Random House, 2001.

Peter Godwin, *When a Crocodile Eats the Sun: A Memoir of Africa*. New York: Little, Brown, 2007.

Nadine Gordimer, *Burger's Daughter*. New York: Viking, 1979.

———, *July's People*. New York: Viking, 1981.

Doris Lessing, *The Grass Is Singing*. London: M. Joseph, 1950.

Rian Malan, *My Traitor's Heart*. London: Bodley Head, 1990.

Nelson Mandela, *Long Walk to Freedom*. Boston: Little, Brown, 1995.

Mark Mathabane, *Kaffir Boy: The True Story of a Black Youth's Coming of Age in Apartheid South Africa*. New York: Macmillan, 1986.

Alan Paton, *Ah, but Your Land Is Beautiful*. New York: Charles Scribner's Sons, 1982.

————, *Too Late the Phalarope*. New York: Charles Scribner's Sons, 1955.

Bibliography

Books

Peter F. Alexander   *Alan Paton: A Biography.* Oxford: Oxford University Press, 1994.

Terry Bell and Dumisa Buhle Ntsebeza   *Unfinished Business: South Africa, Apartheid and Truth.* New York: Verso, 2003.

Alex Boraine   *A Country Unmasked: Inside South Africa's Truth and Reconciliation Commission.* New York: Oxford University Press, 2001.

Horton Davies   "Alan Paton." In *A Mirror of the Ministry in Modern Novels.* New York: Oxford University Press, 1959.

Edmund Fuller   *Books with Men Behind Them.* New York: Random House, 1962.

Harold C. Gardiner   "Why I Liked Some: On Saying 'Boo' to Geese." In *In All Conscience: Reflections on Books and Culture.* Garden City, NY: Hanover House, 1959.

James L. Gibson   *Overcoming Apartheid: Can Truth Reconcile a Divided Nation?* New York: Russell Sage Foundation, 2004.

Anne Paton   *Some Sort of a Job: My Life with Alan Paton.* London: Viking Penguin, 1992.

| Theodore F. Sheckels | "Landmarks." In *The Lion on the Freeway: A Thematic Introduction to Contemporary South African Literature in English.* New York: Peter Lang, 1996. |
| Desmond Tutu | *No Future Without Forgiveness.* New York: Doubleday, 1999. |

Periodicals

Rita Barnard	"Oprah's Paton, or South Africa and the Globalization of Suffering," *English Studies in Africa,* vol. 47, no. 1, 2004.
John H. Chettle	"Africa: Understanding Afrikaners Is Key to Further Reforms," *Wall Street Journal,* November 18, 1985.
Jeremy Cronin	"Post-apartheid South Africa: A Reply to John Saul," *Monthly Review,* December 2002.
Economist	"Special Report: If Only the Adults Would Behave Like the Children—South African Race Relations," April 23, 2005.
Andrew Foley	"'Considered as a Social Record': A Reassessment of *Cry, the Beloved Country*," *English in Africa,* vol. 25, no. 2, October 1998.
Russell J. Linnemann	"Alan Paton: Anachronism or Visionary?" *Commonwealth Novel in English,* Spring/Summer 1984.

Nelson Mandela "Nelson Mandela's Address to the People of Cape Town, Grand Parade, on the Occasion of His Inauguration as State President, 9th May 1994," *Black Scholar*, vol. 24, no. 3, Summer 1994.

Herbert Mitgang "Alan Paton, Author Who Fought Against Apartheid, Is Dead at 85," *New York Times*, April 13, 1988.

Tony Morphet "Alan Paton: The Honour of Meditation," *English in Africa*, December 1983.

Robert Mugabe "Mugabe: 'Snakes in Our Midst,'" *New African*, August/September 2007.

Mueni wa Muiu "'Civilization' on Trial: The Colonial and Postcolonial State in Africa," *Journal of Third World Studies*, vol. 25, no. 1, Spring 2008.

Paul Rich "Liberal Realism in South African Fiction, 1948–1966," *English in Africa*, vol. 12, no. 1, 1985.

Richard Rive "The Liberal Tradition in South African Literature," *Contrast*, July 1983.

Charles Rooney "The Message of Alan Paton," *Catholic World*, November 1961.

Myriam Roson "Interview with Alan Paton," *Crux: A Journal on the Teaching of English*, vol. 21, no. 1, February 1987.

John S. Saul   "Cry for the Beloved Country: The
                    Post-Apartheid Denouement,"
                    Monthly Review, January 2001.

John S. Saul   "Starting from Scratch? A Reply to
                    Jeremy Cronin," *Monthly Review*,
                    December 2002.

Index